SOUTHWEST PASSAGE

JOHN LARDNER

Southwest Passage

THE YANKS IN THE PACIFIC

Introduction by Alex Belth

UNIVERSITY OF NEBRASKA PRESS
LINCOLN AND LONDON

Introduction

When he went off to cover the war in the Pacific in January 1943, John Lardner was twenty-nine years old and, thanks to his weekly column in *Newsweek*, already a major figure in sportswriting. Nothing at Madison Square Garden or Yankee Stadium, however, could match the lure of what awaited him overseas. "The war was everything," he said. "I was glad to be in it, speeding along with it."

Lardner's first stops were Australia and New Guinea, and what he wrote there became the backbone of the book you hold in your hands, *Southwest Passage: The Yanks in the Pacific*. Originally published seventy years ago, this was a buried treasure in Lardner's considerable body of work as a reporter during World War II. It's blessed with Lardner's unmistakable humor, and it captures the immediacy of what was then, to Americans, a new theater of war.

"There was more to be seen, heard, and felt in this war, of course, than the fighting of it," he wrote. "It took Americans to a strange world, with a strange flavor, and gave many of them a long time to look around between bullets."

Lardner crisscrossed Australia for four months, piling

up ten thousand miles as he filed dispatches for the North American Newspaper Alliance and *Newsweek*. A lesser writer may have sought to dramatize what he saw, but Lardner pared away the extraneous with impeccable reporting. In the opening chapter, Lardner writes, "I want to tell the story with as few profundities and earth-shaking conclusions as possible." It's this unpretentious approach to reportage that keeps *Southwest Passage* fresh for us today.

Shortly after he arrived, Lardner observed an American soldier opening diplomatic relations with an Australian in a bar in Sydney.

"Well, boy," said the American, "you can relax now. We're here to save you."

"'Ow is that? I thought you were a fugitive from Pearl Harbor."

About the locals, he wrote: "There can hardly be people in the world more fiercely and fanatically independent than Australians. The notion that the Yanks had come to 'save Australia'–well, some of us had it, sure enough, and there was no quicker way of tasting the quick mettle and genial scorn of the fellow we came to save."

No wonder Orville Prescott of the *New York Times* called *Southwest Passage* "as personal, informal and chatty a book of war correspondence as has yet come along. Mr. Lardner has the happy faculty of taking the war seriously without taking himself seriously."

Lardner's equanimity came naturally. He was, after all,

the son of Ring Lardner, who was America's most famous sportswriter before he became its most famous literary wit. Like his father, the son was serious about writing. As he said in a letter home: "It seems pretty plain that the best thing to do during the war is to work hard at whatever work you have to do, wherever it may be. Working is the only way I've ever found of being happy in a bad time."

Lardner had been witness to the pitfalls of being labeled a sportswriter. His father never fully escaped being typecast as *just* a sportswriter. But John wasn't just a sportswriter; he was one of the best. His reputation was cemented when he began a *True* magazine piece about a hell-bent prizefighter with these words: "Stanley Ketchel was twenty-four when he was fatally shot in the back by the common-law husband of the lady who was cooking his breakfast." Lardner's fellow sportswriting legend Red Smith called it the "greatest novel ever written in one sentence."

Like his contemporaries W. C. Heinz and A. J. Liebling, Lardner was a war correspondent, and if he didn't enjoy their longevity or the lasting renown of Smith or Jimmy Cannon, he was every bit their equal. Heinz, in fact, is on record as calling Lardner "the best."

"Time has a way of dimming the memory and achievements of writers who wrote, essentially, for the moment, as writers writing for journals must do," Ira Berkow, a longtime columnist of the *New York Times*, told me. "But the best shouldn't be lost in the haze of history and John Lardner was a brilliant writer–which means, in my view, that he was insightful, irreverent, wry and a master of English prose."

John was born in 1912, the first of Ring and Ellis Lardner's four boys. Their father was a study in reserve, a poker-faced observer of human folly who ushered his sons into the family business, although not by design. When his third son, Ring Jr., sold his first magazine piece, the father said, "Good God, isn't any one of you going to turn out to be anything but a writer?"

The Lardners moved to the East Coast from Chicago in the fall of 1919. Early on, they lived in Great Neck, Long Island, the model for the fictional West Egg in F. Scott Fitzgerald's *The Great Gatsby* (for a time, Fitzgerald was one of Ring's closest friends). Another friend was Grantland Rice, who succeeded Lardner as the most celebrated sportswriter in the country. Whenever Ring took his sons to Yankee Stadium, Babe Ruth and Lou Gehrig always came by to pay their respects.

In his memoir, *The Lardners: My Family Remembered*, Ring Jr. wrote about the striking similarities he and his brothers shared with their father: "Intellectual curiosity with a distinctly verbal orientation, taciturnity, a lack of emotional display, an appreciation of the ridiculous. It was a matter of course that you mastered the fundamentals of reading and writing at the age of four, and by six reading books was practically a full-time occupation."

John was all of ten when he broke into print with this ditty for the *New York World*:

Babe Ruth and old Jack Dempsey,
Both sultans of the swat
One hits where other people are,
The other where they're not.

Ring Jr. claimed that John, more than any of his brothers, patterned his life on his father's. John was bright and restless, and perhaps he pushed himself because he didn't want to be known only as Ring's son. He wasn't given to talking about his motivations, but it is no stretch to assume that his father's considerable talent gave him something to shoot for.

"John grew up in the shadow of a father who was a great writer," Liebling wrote. "This is a handicap shared by only an infinitesimal portion of any given generation, but it did not intimidate him."

As for himself, John wrote, "In the interests of learning to read and cipher, I made the rounds at a number of schools, my tour culminating in Phillips Academy, Andover, and Harvard University (one year), where I picked up the word 'culminating.'"

He went to Paris for another year to study at the Sorbonne, worked for a few months in Paris on the *International Herald Tribune*, then returned to New York in 1931 and landed a job with the *New York Herald Tribune*. He covered local news and quickly earned bylines–no small achievement at what was considered the city's best-written paper. "We are all swollen up like my ankles," his father boasted.

At twenty-one, John left the *Herald Tribune* to write a column for the North American Newspaper Alliance. It was the Depression, and he was pulling down an impressive $100 a week, but his father would not live long enough to see him cash any paychecks. Ring died in 1933 after suffering for years from tuberculosis and alcoholism. He was forty-eight.

In the late '30s, John began his transition to magazine writing. He published a story for the *Saturday Evening Post* on the Black Sox scandal and launched the *Newsweek* sports column that would run for eighteen years and establish his reputation. And yet, for all of that, the rumblings of the coming war were impossible to ignore.

Finally, in 1940, he wrote a letter to John Wheeler, his boss at NANA:

> A year or so ago you suggested–not at all in a definitive
> way, but simply as something to think about–that in case
> of real action abroad, perhaps involving this country, you
> might consider sending me to do some work there in-
> stead of, or in addition to, the people that usually do the
> stuff of that kind for you and the *Times*. The idea stuck
> in my mind, naturally, but I haven't given it any serious

thought until recently. I think I can do other work as well as or better than most newspaper men and writers, and that a time may be coming shortly when that work will be more important and valuable to both you and me. This sounds swellheaded–but if I didn't feel the way I do about writing, I wouldn't give a damn about being a writer.

John got his wish not long after the Japanese bombed Pearl Harbor. During his voyage to Australia he wrote to his wife, Hazel: "I have now stated for the 143rd time that I don't think Billy Conn can beat Joe Louis. This opinion is not censorable, and I will pass it along to you, too, for what it is worth, though you probably knew it all the time."

Lardner traveled with four other American reporters during his twelve weeks in Australia. All proved more than happy to break up their considerable downtime by arguing about the following: "Food; Russia; women; the Louis-Schemling fights; the art of Michelangelo; the Civil War; religion; the Newspaper Guild; Cornelia Otis Skinner; tattooing; the best place to live in New England; William Randolph Hearst; war production; venereal disease; the Pyramids; walking-sticks; dining out as opposed to dining home; the private life of Hedy Lamarr; marriage; *For Whom the Bell Tolls*; prizefight managers; education for children; Enzo Fiermonte; Paris; this war and all others; Leopold and Loeb; San Francisco restaurants; Greek and Roman architecture; Seabiscuit; the comparative merits of Cleopatra and Mary Queen of Scots. And several hundred others."

As consistently amusing as Lardner is in *Southwest Passage*, he strives for more than comic effect in his dispatches. Take his description of Darwin, the ghost town "at the topmost pole of the dusty road across Australia, brooding over its scars"; or his account of the nurses who survived brutal air raids in the Philippines with "their hard-bought shell of resistance." Nothing showy, nothing fancy–just a world-class observer at work, as Lardner was when he encountered a swing band performing for a U.S. Army outfit near Darwin a few days after Easter. "The night, following a day without bombs, was moonlit, and the Southern Cross blazed above. The musicians brought their guns as well as their instruments."

Lardner downplayed any personal jeopardy he faced, but as Liebling said, "John was naturally brave. When he saw blinding bomb flashes by night, he used to move *toward* them to see better." Lardner himself might have chalked that up to poor eyesight, but his courage is evidenced by his trip through hostile waters to Port Moresby on a freighter dubbed the "Floating Firecracker," whose cargo consisted of bombs and drums of gasoline. On another occasion, after successfully bombing their target off the north coast of New Guinea, the plane Lardner was aboard stopped to refuel at a barren little base. The men ate bread and marmalade in the mess shack while Lardner talked to one of the soldiers about the ice hockey playoffs for the Stanley Cup.

We got our last thrill of the day then, thrown in for good measure and absolutely unsolicited. Doggedly the Zeros [Japanese fighter planes] had trailed us south, and with them came bombers. The alarm sounded, and the crews on the ground beelined for their planes, for there is nothing more humiliating, useless, and downright impractical than to be caught on the ground, in the open, with your aeronautical pants down.

There is nothing more scary, I should add, because something always goes a little wrong when you try to take off under the condition known as "or else." One of the engines missed. Then the door failed to shut tight . . . but we did get off, after sitting there for what seemed like a couple of minutes longer than forever.

Given his natural reticence, there is little to be found in Lardner's papers revealing his feelings about *Southwest Passage*. In letters home he didn't much talk about himself or the content of his work, just the conditions under which he produced it. "As far as I know the stories I've been writing have not been done by others," he wrote to his wife. "The main trouble with being frontward and one of the reasons I'll have to spend more time here is communications and censorship. You can't be sure how fast your stuff is getting to headquarters and clearing from there, and you have no way of knowing what's being taken out of stories. It's like writing in a void."

Lardner came home to resume his sports column in the

summer of 1942, but by the end of the year he was a war correspondent again. His first stops were North Africa and Italy, then it was back to the Pacific, where he went ashore at Iwo Jima only a few hours after the first wave of marines. By the time he covered the invasion of Okinawa, now also writing for the *New Yorker*, he was haunted by the deaths of two of his brothers: Jim was the last American volunteer to die in the Spanish Civil War, in 1938, and David was killed in 1944 by a landmine in France. You can practically feel the shadow of mortality on him in the letter he wrote to his wife after filing his dispatch from Okinawa: "That was the last one, baby. During the last few days I was there, I got one or two small and gentle hints, much more gentle than the one at Iwo Jima, that my luck was beginning to run out and I had better quit while I was still in one hand-some, symmetrical piece. By the time I get home it will be practically three and a half years since I started covering the war which I guess will be enough."

Like his father, John had considerable health problems for much of his adult life: TB, heart disease, and multiple sclerosis. Undeterred, he worked hard and steadily as he gave up his syndicated newspaper column to write long magazine pieces for *True* and *Sport* as well as the *New Yorker*. Along the way he published two collections of his columns, *It Beats Working* and *Strong Cigars and Lovely Women*, and a history of the golden age of boxing called *White Hopes and Other Tigers*.

A certain mystique rose up around Lardner. He was forever described as someone who could stay at the bar all
evening, nursing a Scotch, smoking, and scarcely saying
a word. "He was as easy to like as he was hard to know,"
said Liebling. And yet he was far from morose. "I'd like
to fend off at least a few tragic overtones in the account
of John Lardner," his daughter Susan once wrote. "Those
of us who knew my father . . . remember him as a song-
singing, piano-playing, butter pecan ice cream–eating cat
rancher and driver of Buick convertibles, who drank more
milk than whisky and who often and rightly referred to
himself as Handsome Jack."

John had always told friends he wouldn't outlive his old
man, and he was right. He died of a heart attack in 1960
six weeks before his forty-eighth birthday. That day, he was
writing an obituary for an old family friend, Franklin P.
Adams. "F.P.A. was always a poor poker player and often a
bore," he wrote before collapsing with chest pains. When
the family doctor arrived, he took Lardner in his arms and
said, "John, you can't die. John, you're a noble human
being." Lardner looked at him and said, "Oh Lou, that
sounds like a quotation."

In September of 1943, Lardner sat down in a stone house
in southern Italy to compose his latest dispatch from the
war. He had written in less commodious surroundings as
he bounced from Australia to New Guinea to North Africa,

but he neither complained about them nor reveled in this rare taste of comfort. Usually he was glad for mail call, too, even if it came in midsentence. But not this day.

Lardner was hoping for a letter from his wife and instead received a legal notice from the midwestern law firm of Duffy, Claffy, Igoe & McCorkindale. The letter concerned a column he had written about a former outfielder from St. Louis named Bohnsack, who seemed not to have been memorable except that he once threw an umpire off a moving train. Lardner, who knew something worth writing about when he saw it, happily included the incident in his column. Now Bohnsack's lawyers were claiming the anecdote was "false and misleading," and they urged Lardner to settle out of court. Then as now, there was nothing like a little moola to ease a fellow's "grievous social and mental damage."

Lardner seethed: "Bohnsack annoyed me because he showed me that his world, which had also been my world, had great vitality, and that it took considerably more than a global battle to kill its self-preoccupation," he wrote. It wasn't just that Bohnsack had told Lardner personally that he'd thrown the umpire off a train, or that the first piece of mail he had received in the battle zone was not from his wife. "It was most of all that now, in the midst of the great and bloody planetary adventure of war, these barristers chose callously to call me back to the world of petulant outfielders and remind me that I was a sports writer."

In fact, Lardner wrote about a variety of topics: lexicography, jury service, and New York history; for the *New Yorker* he contributed occasional film, theater, and book reviews and in the last three and a half years of his life wrote a column for the magazine on TV and radio. "Sportswriter" was a label that he, like his father, would never escape. This slim volume of his war reportage proves that Lardner was a quick-witted and assured writer no matter the subject. As Stanley Walker, the *Herald Tribune*'s city editor, said, Lardner "came close to being the perfect all-around journalist." Never were those skills put to a stiffer test than on the battlefields in Europe and the Pacific. In the thickest drama, the unflappable man remained unflappable, at his best writing what Red Smith called novels in a single sentence.

CONTENTS

CHAPTER		PAGE
I	THE UNREADY	11
II	~~WESTWARD~~ (CENSORED) HO! . .	17
III	CONVOY	22
IV	ALL ASHORE	37
V	THE SHIRTSLEEVE BAEDEKER . .	44
VI	THE LAST BASTION	60
VII	MACARTHUR AND MACARTHURIANA .	72
VIII	ROAD COMPANY	82
IX	DARWIN	89
X	JAPS, MOSTLY DEAD	105
XI	THE PLANES WE FIGHT WITH . .	112
XII	DAKOTA IN THE RED DUST . . .	122
XIII	AS THE DUTCHMAN FLIES . . .	133
XIV	CITY LIFE	144
XV	LOG OF THE *FIRECRACKER* . .	158
XVI	PORT OF BOMBS AND BUTTERFLIES .	170
XVII	BETWEEN ZEROS	189
XVIII	SEVEN DEADLY YOUNG MEN . .	202

CHAPTER		PAGE
XIX	CORAL SEA	211
XX	DIGGERS AT WORK	224
XXI	BEHIND THE LINES	241
XXII	THE TASMAN BUMPS	259
XXIII	HOMEWARD: THE ODD PACE . .	275
NOTES .	. . . .	291
GLOSSARY	. . . .	298

SOUTHWEST PASSAGE

I

The Unready

THE first time I saw a machine gun fired by Americans in this war, it didn't work. The first time I saw an anti-aircraft gun leveled for loading, it had a broken train. The first time I saw a naval gun prepared for aiming, it didn't get aimed—because the gunnery officer called a range that the men in the gun crew couldn't find on the gun.

It may not have been the officer's fault. The "talker" on the bridge may have called the wrong figure over his head-phone. It was the "talker's" first experience in battle action. For that matter, it was the officer's first experience, and the crew's. For that matter, there was no action. The alarm signal of "Battle Stations!" had rung in our ears by mistake, because a kid sending signals from out on the edge of the convoy had mixed up his flags.

For that matter . . .

Well, for that matter, three newspaper men started to get on the wrong ship the night our convoy sailed, and a steward shooed us off with deep contempt and a diagram showing that our cabin numbers did not match his vessel and never would. Then a buck private, dizzied by the mystery of where he and the rest of us were going and loath to put up with further riddles, demanded to know whether the big white "*C*" on the armband of my uniform stood for "Canadian" or "Cop." He had never seen anything like it. Neither had anyone else.

The "C" stood for "correspondent." We were a raffish lot to look at, the correspondents, the first to step forth in the regalia of the United States Army, with bedrolls and head-nets and canteens and revolver belts with no revolvers, to sail with a task force to a foreign land. We were of a piece with the rest of the picture: the picture of a country and an army and a navy at war but innocent of knowledge of war, full of fight but uncertain how to flex a fist, earnest, awkward, stumbling, getting up and falling down again, learning from day to day and learning always the hard way—aware of potential might and resources to come, but aware too of the crying needs and desperate lacks of the moment.

My conscience done told me, when I was in knee-pants: don't be a typewriter strategist * or a shift-key solon. If I break that grave commandment for an instant, it is only to remark how swiftly a given nation can unlearn war, and lose the uses, reflexes, and very

* Note 1, page 291.

feel of war, when all around it the craft is reaching its highest state of cultivation.

That's how it seemed at the start. In the next few months, we began catching up. Those were the months I spent in the Southwest Pacific, the first field of battle, when America's war was young.

Troops and correspondents alike, we sailed off blindfold, not knowing our destination. We came to Australia, and there we broke up and spread out to see new things and taste the new war and learn about it. On planes, railroads, ships, and trucks I traveled around Australia and into New Guinea and over the green seas that lie between. I saw Dutchmen dispossessed and fugitive, and Australians gathering from distant battlefields to resist invasion of their home, and Americans rushed to the help of these outposts of our own defense. I saw airmen giving and taking the first blows, finding out how well they could fight and also finding out that their pursuit planes, so highly thought of back in the States, were not as good as the enemy's planes. This was harsh for a first lesson; but not so harsh as the first lesson of the homegrown Australian air force which bucked the Jap in a slow little trainer called the Wirraway.

In some respects, the Wirraway and the men who flew it were symbols of the early Pacific war: the unready and peace-loving against the swift, hungry, and prepared. We had no planes in the Philippines because they were shattered on the ground. The Australians had this plane—and when the enemy came to Timor and New Britain and New Guinea, the Australians went up to meet them in the Wirraway, and each man went knowing what the chances were. But he went.

It was better when American pursuit planes reached the Southwest Pacific, and it will be still better when those and other weapons are supplanted by still better ones. We did what we could with the tools at hand, in the early weeks of defensive war. I saw our best improve as time went by. I saw our bombers begin to smash Japanese ships, fields, and bases, and I saw ground gunners—some of whom were still struggling to learn their jobs with stiff new machine guns on the voyage from home—begin to nail Japanese planes on the wing.

There was more to be seen, heard, and felt in this war, of course, than the fighting of it. It took Americans to a strange world, with a strange flavor, and gave many of them a long time to look around between bullets. Life in this war, as in other wars, was a little of everything: the mosquitoes of Port Moresby, the flies of Alice Springs, the sharks of the Coral Sea coming up for refuse; a soldiers' band concert in the night in the jungle of Darwin; mass wassail at Lennon's Hotel in Brisbane; the tiny Toonerville train that ran across

Australia's barren core; New England boiled dinner on a freighter loaded with bombs and airplane fuel; the crowds outside General MacArthur's hotel; brawls in Melbourne, and murder by an American private; crap games and racing and lotteries; politicians inspecting troops; gin and limejuice in the smothering heat of a tropical rainstorm, while the phonograph played "Franklin D. Roosevelt Jones."

Those things, the young war in the Southwest Pacific and its background, were as fresh and strange to me, coming from Yankee Stadium, Jacobs Beach, and Madison Square Garden, as they were to the first private to leave the Dakota prairieland for Australia. I want to tell the story with as few profundities and earth-shaking conclusions as possible—though a war correspondent finds it harder to resist drawing conclusions than drawing two cards to a three-card flush (and I am looking straight at my fellow-members of the Coral Sea & Barrier Reef Nightly Poker Club, maximum speed, 11 knots).

Americans at home have been kidded with great regularity by Congressmen and by catchwords and by characters with pink glasses on their eyes or sinister motives in their hearts. Everything I saw on the western wing of our battlefront indicated that the war there will be hard and for keeps. So far our men under arms have learned and fought at the same time, but every day we have less to learn and more skill to give to the ancient pastime our enemies have studied to perpetuate. We have come to realize that wars are not won by production alone—they are won by (*a*) wanting to win, plus (*b*) knowing how, plus (*c*) production.

I think what I watched in the first few months of the war, against a backdrop of strange cities and desert and jungle and green water, was America in the throes of adding together (*a*) and (*b*) and (*c*).

II

~~Westward~~ (Censored) Ho!

"IF we're going to Australia, the beer is warm," said Kirkland, a large cameraman who had been there.

"What if we don't go to Australia?" I asked him.

Kirk scratched his brown mustache with a thumbnail.

"If we don't go there, I don't know how the hell the beer is," he admitted.

The problem for troops, officers, and hitchhiking reporters was twofold:

1. Where are we going?
2. If we're going to Australia, where and what is it?

The second question could be subdivided:

2a. Will we make it?

This was the first large troop convoy to sail west since America's declaration of war. After the quick disaster of Pearl Harbor and the fall of Manila and the start of our desperate stand on Bataan peninsula in the Philippines, the battle stood suspended for us at home and left us to scramble. In the mass, the country was like a freshly recruited, one-truck fire department facing its first fire.

There were firemen still in bed, knuckling the sleep from their eyes. There were firemen grabbing for their pants and pulling them on. There were firemen sliding down the pole, and firemen dashing around the truck in circles, yelling to know where the fire was and what to do about it and who was going to drive the blank blank truck, if the truck worked.

For the troops we sailed with, the task was simplified. No matter how new the war, how ragged the preparation, how strange the work, they had been chosen and they were going—some leader somewhere above them knew where. They marched early. If they left confusion behind them, their own lives were caught up in one plain, immediate purpose: to go where the enemy was and to fight him and beat him.

Naturally, they speculated on where, how, and when. They had time to speculate.

Some of our troops were Negroes, stevedore troops, the first to leave the country. Ninety-five per cent of them had never seen an ocean before (the percentage among the white troops was scarcely less). With the world in a state of bloody flux, from Oceania west to the Atlantic sea lanes, we might be going to Australia and we might not. It was a possibility, noised about, and a colored private, first-class, who stood by the rail on our first day out took cognizance of it.

"Whereabouts is Australia, Wilfred?" he said.

"I guess it's somewhere in Africa," said his neighbor; then shook his head and turned an eye full of frank admiration on the sea. "Look at them waves, the way they get green when they fold over!"

One company smuggled its mascot aboard the ship, a part-way police dog named Dopey, who huddled silent, like a tested conspirator, when he passed up the gangway in a dufflebag beneath the eyes and ears of the officers on duty. The dog was challenging destiny and a can of chloroform, for Australia, free of hydrophobia, rejects all alien hounds at her door. But none of us knew this, not knowing to begin with that Australia was our goal.

The men of the convoy, still rough around the edges and awkward in their new life, did not know that they would be hailed in Australia for courtliness and polished grace of manner—so many Chesterfields on the hoof. They did not know the soldier who would make them seem so by contrast, the Digger—rough, free product of an uncongested life, justly annoyed by the "bloody pleases" and "bloody thank you's" of the Yank, ready to give the shirt off his back or to take the shirt off another's, a kidder, a fighter, a gay desperado, and the best physical specimen of soldier in the world.

Private *B*. Lynch was downright blissful in his ignorance. Australia wrecked the peace of mind of *B*. Lynch the moment he got there. As his first gesture of free will in the State of Queensland, the private bought a lottery ticket. The radio announced him as the winner of 6,000 pounds, Australian, and his heels were still in midair in a joyous kick when Corporal *D*. Lynch, of the Australian army, stepped forward with the winning ticket.

B. Lynch did not know how happy he was with us on shipboard, touching his toes in the morning, trotting to boat drill in the afternoon, and losing nickels at blackjack in the gloaming.

But then, nobody knew anything. As Kirk said, the beer is warm if we go to Australia. Otherwise...

Recently I read the proofs of the new Army guidebook for soldiers Australia-bound. We had no guidebooks. We did have Hutch, the purser, who rode those ships and those waters in the days when Doris Duke, in a gaudy cabin forward on the port side, was the star passenger of the Hawaii run and a purser was a seagoing Ward McAllister.

Hutch had a weakness for reciting Kipling to defenseless soldiers, but he did know something of Australia, and he wrote a table of Australian coinage for the troops and a glossary of Australian slang—just in case. The boys were interested to hear that "bastard," pronounced "bahs-tud," was a term of endearment.

"But only in Australia," warned the purser. "And

God knows if we're going there—God and the character who steers this convoy."

For a man of an intellectual, a spiritual turn of mind, there was only one thing to be done in the circumstances. I made book. Soldiers, officers, crewmen, correspondents—cash customers of any description—could weigh the odds, as posted on a cabin wall, under the general heading of "Whither are we drifting?":

> Perth—3 to 1.
> Darwin—6 to 1.
> Pago Pago—12 to 1.
> Adelaide—4 to 1.
> Little America—50 to 1.
> Grand Central Station, Upper Level—75 to 1.
> Brisbane—11 to 5.
> Nome—30 to 1.
> Sydney—5 to 1.
> Pittsburgh—100 to 1.
> Tokyo—25 to 1.

I did get one bet on Pittsburgh, from a captain in the Quartermaster Corps.

"I've just been shot in the arm for yellow fever and three times for typhus," he said with a scowl, "and I don't think they have 'em in Pittsburgh. But I never passed up a hundred-to-one shot in my life. Here's a buck."

III

Convoy

THE men boarded swiftly in the semi-dark, lugging
their gear. They were the first to take the new helmets
abroad, low over the brow, ears, and nape of the neck,
like the German and Japanese helmets. Issued the day
before, these hump-backed hats were strange and grotesque to eyes accustomed to the old flat model.

The silence was broken only by shuffling feet and
the shouts of officers that sounded hollow through the
long reaches of the covered pier.

"When I call your last name, answer with your first
name! All right. Brown?"

"Here."

"____ ____ ____ ____! Answer with your first
name! Brown?"

"Herbert."

"Okay. Move along."

They filed aboard the ships, marching to war. There
were thousands of them, and the hours of the night
passed by, dim and unreal, and the shuffle of feet con-
tinued. Once aboard, the men found their bunks in the

crowded cabins, saloons, and deckways, and went to sleep. It was not a night to lie in the dark and think of the future. The day had been too hard. When their backs hit the bedding, they slept.

Later the transports and their escorts slipped out to sea. On the second night, our ship scraped an enemy submarine. It was our only meeting of the voyage with the agents of Tojo, and no one knew about it but the watch. The captain spoke of it a few days afterward.

"Damn near rammed him full," he said. "At that, we may have hurt him some. No, it wasn't any whale."

One day was enough to accustom the men to the routine of this voyage to an unknown destination—the time and whereabouts of mess, the setting-up drill on deck in the morning, the abandon-ship drill in the afternoon, visits to the hospital in the old ship's bar for shots in the arm, the places where a soldier was allowed to go and those where he wasn't.

The card games—bridge, poker, hearts, blackjack—quickly crystallized among certain groups at certain hours. Here and there a soldier had a map, and became the center of a navigation forum; pins and pencil marks plotted our course on a dozen different charts, and no two schools of thought agreed exactly on any given day. The guy up there on the bridge, who knew, wasn't talking.

I will have to state that our own course—the corre-

spondents' course, as plotted on the correspondents'
chart, up forward on the port side, by Lewis B. Sebring,
of the *New York Herald Tribune*—was a pretty good
one, one of the best. Sebring played to good houses
daily, matinée and evening. The officers of the ship
came around to look at his pins and learn where the
hell Sebring thought we were.

They seemed to get much manly merriment out of
this pastime, but Sebring was not disturbed. A bachelor
and a precisionist, he had a gift with those pins, and
when in the end I discovered how close he was, I for-
gave the fellow for his ghoulish desk work eleven years
before, when we worked on the same paper and he
assigned me nothing but two-paragraph obits. Time
heals all wounds.

There's a way of navigating at sea which appeals to
landlubbers, once they discover it. You take a watch
and a matchstick and line up the match's shadow with
the hour hand. You bisect the angle between the
shadow and the figure 12 on the watch, and what you
get is South. That is, it's South if you live clean and do
not develop the shakes.

Matchstick navigation became epidemic, as we
plowed through the blue Pacific. Even the Commanding Officer of the troops in convoy went in for it. He
lined up South once on his watch and then lined it up
again.

"The trouble is, Ben," said the C.O. to his adjutant, "it's a different direction each time."

"That's because the ship is zig-zagging," said the adjutant.

"Oh, fine," said the C.O. "Then I'll calculate South on the zig and then on the zag and strike an average."

Which he did, with much simple pleasure.

The C.O. was an officer who won his men quickly and completely—Brigadier General Frank S. Clark, veteran artilleryman from Massachusetts, recently commandant of the Coast Artillery School at Fort Monroe, Va. A trim little man with a gray mustache, he was mild of manner but firm in command and deceptively shrewd.

Soon after we sailed, the general censored the bill-of-fare. Men and officers were eating luxury cruise rations, in quantities that shocked the general. He ran his blue pencil through passion-fruit juice and squab and much of the rest of it.

"Let's have honest victuals in honest amounts," he said.

The best eaters aboard were young doctors of the Medical Corps. As former manager of a stable of eaters, ranging from bantamweight to heavyweight, that swept the field in special matches along Broadway in the years 1933-38, I am qualified to say that a medical man relaxing at sea yields to nobody in speed and capacity at the trough.

The doctors did not relax completely, though. There was work to do, fourteen victims of seasickness, stomach-ache, and minor cuts and abrasions the first day out, "splendid practice," as the general called it. More than that, the men of the Medical Corps were looking forward eagerly to their job in the Southwest Pacific, boning up on tropical medicine from their books in the medical library.

The medical library, brought aboard by loving hands, was situated in the ship's hospital, and the hospital, as I said before, was in the old bar, below and aft. There the doctors stowed their books on a shelf where the barkeep once planted his vermouth and grenadine and bitters. In the icebox back of the bar, where high-priced ale used to flourish, the doctors cooled fruit juice and Pepsi-Cola for the use of soldiers who needed a chaser after a shot of anti-tetanus or anti-typhus.

It was strictly saloon service, the way we took those shots. The hospital was a bright box of equatorial heat, shut off from the blacked-out deck by doors that were tightly closed at night. We stepped up in turn—men, officers, correspondents—put our feet on the old brass rail, and rested our elbows on the bar, shirtless or with

sleeves rolled up to the shoulder. Then the bartender
went to work on our orders, with his gleaming needle
and his cotton swab.

The bartender was Captain S. A. Spencer, the transport surgeon, once a football player. He was big and
blond, naked to the waist, always grinning. He was undoubtedly the most efficient man who ever served that
bar.

From the old vermouth nook, the library, a medical
major drew one of three fat red-backed volumes that
stood side by side.

"This is Volume Two of Strong's revision of Stitt's
*Diagnosis, Prevention, and Treatment of Tropical
Diseases,*" he announced. "Some of us know damn little about tropical medicine. We're cramming, making
digests. For instance, snakebite. Here's the digest:
'There are many snakes in certain parts of Australia,
some of which are poisonous. The poisonous ones belong either to the sea-snake group, which have an eel-
shaped tail and a rather flattened body, or' " . . .

"When did you hear we were going to Australia,
Doc?" asked a soldier, rolling up his sleeve. "Did that
come out in the evening papers?"

"I'm just playing it safe," said the major.

"The sea-snake," said your correspondent didacti-
cally, being a herpetologist in a small way, "has a venom

of high toxic content, but is a lousy biter, on account of his short teeth and small head."

"That so?" said the soldier, moving up to the bar. "Well, I hope he tries you first, with one of them lousy bites."

Sometimes, as you look over the rolling ocean toward the horizon, you see planes—if your mind is on planes. All of us, naturally, had planes and submarines on our minds some of the time. Joe Dearing, cameraman from San Francisco, pointed suddenly from the rail one day at the sky low off our starboard beam.

"Look at 'em come!" he shouted. "Those planes there. There must be a hundred of 'em."

Even the sharp-eyed soldiers on watch were deceived, like Joe and the rest of us, for a moment. And it was actually a matter of a few minutes before those black specks on the horizon, that seemed to fly at us in formation, resolved themselves in our eyes into what they were—a strange cloud pattern, a trick of sun, sky, and shadow.

The real planes we saw were our own. They were observation planes, scanning our patch of ocean mile by mile, often disappearing from view in their long and steady patrol. A cruiser catapulted them into the air, and when they returned from the job, they came to light by the cruiser's side, and the mother ship reached out with her crane and derricked them back to her bosom again.

Young soldiers manned our anti-aircraft guns. We watched the machine guns loaded, every fifth round a red tracer bullet, and watched them fired for the first time. The war was new, and so were the guns, and most of them had bugs in them—wouldn't work the first time. But they worked soon enough, smoothly and sharply. The gunners took plenty of practice. Between-times, standing their guns in shifts, they talked of the weapons they itched to use against the enemy.

"MacArthur's gunners get good results with Jap planes, the way it looks," said a corporal. The Americans in Bataan were making history then.

"I'll tell you," said the lieutenant behind him. "You can bring down planes with machine-gun ack-ack, all right, if you stick to the guns. There's a tendency to leave a gun too soon, to flinch away or duck, when a plane dives in your direction. You have to stick to the gun and keep it blazing. I figure that's what MacArthur's gunners are doing."

The Navy handled its own big guns, and the signal system, for the Navy was in charge of the convoy. A stern disciplinarian was Ensign James Austin "Fearless" Parks, commanding the signal crew on our ship.

"If a guy misses a signal," said Ensign Parks ferociously, "I make him go down and study the book for half an hour."

Ensign Parks was the Pacific Ocean's foremost Brooklyn Dodger fan, a native of Brooklyn, and a graduate of Fordham. In the Navy he was like a hawk in a chicken yard.

"Because of the following reason," said Ensign Parks, "I know Notre Dame can't be licked in football. That is a truism. My commission brings me among these suckers who are always betting on Navy in football. Misguided. 'Jim,' I remark to myself, Jim being my name, 'this is the promised land.' Oh, my, how I clip these philistines on the Navy-Notre Dame game!" yelled Ensign Parks.

"You seem in particularly high fettle this morning, Fearless," said Ensign John "Seaweed" Drake, the gunnery officer, fully as young as Parks.

"Me?" said Ensign Parks. "Certainly. Ain't you jolly? I'm a jolly fellow, happy as the day is long."

Parks's poker was only fair, however. It reduced his jolliness. It sometimes depressed him to a point where he could scarcely be heard two decks away.

There was no better poker player on the ship, even among the sergeants, than Martin Barnett, plump Paramount Newsreel man. Barnett was also a better casino player than I was, and the proprietor of the only pneumatic-bedroll-with-a-foot-pump on board, and the largest supply of salt-water soap, which he tried in vain to sell at a discount. You don't want much salt-water soap. You use as little as you have to. With fresh water limited to drinking purposes, we all had to shave and bathe in salt water—but we saved soap on laundry. Land-based laundering is better than sea-based, the same as with airplanes. A soldier or correspondent might as well wash his clothes in ground glass as in salt water.

We lived five to a cabin—but not when the High Seas Hillbillies went to work with close harmony. The Hill-billies—consisting of Barnett, Carleton V. Kent, of the *Chicago Times,* and myself—could empty a cabin faster than the call to "Battle Stations." It was not bad singing either, with the swipes we developed in *Moonlight Bay* and *Mandy Lee*. It was certainly not so bad as Hutch, the purser, reciting *Boots, Boots, Boots.*

We sometimes sang above decks, in the tropic moon, till driven below again by popular mandate.

Jack Turcott, eyes and ears of Captain Joe Patterson's *New York Daily News,* was an over-strong banjo player. As soon as he broke the strings of one banjo with his hot treatment of *Christopher Columbo,* Turcott would sift among the troops in search of another. He never wrecked a banjo without returning it promptly to its owner, with words of friendly advice that came from his long experience with banjos.

"If you keep this thing in a dry place," said Turcott, in the middle of the wet Pacific, "the strings will last longer."

The transport that slid along beside us, on the port side, was giving off a rattle of machine-gun fire when the first Sunday religious services were held on our ship. Behind a plain table flanked by the American flag and the Army church flag stood the chaplain, Colonel Edwin C. Cooke. He was tall, dark, and spare, and strong enough to dominate the wild confusion about him: the wind howling topside, the crackle of our neighbor's gunfire as she tested her .50's across a brief stretch of water, and the tramp of feet far down the deck where soldiers were doing calisthenics. Drill ended when services began, no sooner.

"Testing, testing!"

The chaplain's voice was metallic over the loud-speaker. Order emerged from chaos on deck, though the wind still whistled and the nearby guns still spoke sporadically. Eight Negro soldiers, a double quartette, filed in shy procession up to the table and took their places around the microphone. Haltingly, they sang the first notes of *Swing Low, Sweet Chariot*. The microphone played tricks on them, the lead singer was low-voiced, and the bass was nervous, almost inaudible at first. But the song grew stronger as the singers heard themselves through the wind and took courage.

The second chorus was clear and eloquent, and filled the deck with music. Then the singers shuffled away, losing themselves quietly in the rows of men that faced the table and the flags. The chaplain read the 103rd Psalm. He delivered the sermon, short and forceful. He prayed, and when it was over, the men broke ranks at their officers' commands and threaded their way back to quarters.

Between our first Sunday at sea and our last, there were days and nights of remorseless heat. I spent one evening sitting in a circle of enlisted men, in the space between two tiers of bunks, talking about prizefights and baseball. We drank pop from half-cooled bottles, and the sweat rolled over our chins and down our chests in little rivers. There were dozens of these meetings, all over the ship, every night—usually at a certain time, fixed informally by the soldiers of each group. One by one they dropped into place in the circle when the appointed time came and began to talk. An hour or so later they would drop out, one by one, and go to their bunks. There was no reading at night, in quarters. No lights burned.

One night the heat eased off, and the next day a cool wild wind picked up our trail and followed us all the way into Australia.

We didn't always know what happened in our convoy. There was a morning, in the dark, early hours, when an alarm of "enemy vessels sighted" reached the men on the bridge and sent the night watch rushing to guns and stations. We heard about it only next day. It was a false alarm.

There was an alarm of sorts, too, when the dog Dopey, mascot of the Negro troops, was kidnaped and hidden a couple of days before we reached port. Dopey was kidnaped by his masters, at the hour scheduled for his execution as an undesirable alien to whom the land of Australia was forbidden. The military police found him at last, under a soldier's bunk below, and returned him to the deathhouse.

Kent and I were sitting in the cabin of the ship's chief officer when the dog was found. A seaman with a lugubrious face entered the room, bearing a tray with a small can in the middle of it.

"What are you weeping about?" the chief snapped at the seaman.

Then his eye fell on the can, and he swallowed twice and turned slightly pale.

"So the Army is passing the buck to me," he said bitterly. "I have to kill animals now."

Under the circumstances, it was the easiest sort of diplomatic dodge for us to persuade the chief and the Army to compromise. The troops raised a pool to pay

Dopey's freight back to America, and the dog's life was spared. He deserved the reprieve. The voyage was no plan of his.

One day out of Australia, with the name of our goal now an open secret, excitement ran high—and so did the wind. At this time of all times the ship ran full into the worst storm in her captain's experience, and the men, weary of the wastes of water, saw more water than they had ever dreamed of.

The guns were lashed. Troops were ordered off the decks. Then the storm hurled us into a trough from behind, canceling our steering. We had to turn on our screws and head back into the wind. There was no visibility. The wind whipped the ship, and smashed the davits of our lifeboats. Portholes were broken and water rushed in, sweeping one cabinful of airplane technicians into the corridor. The doctors had their hands full with cuts and bruises next day.

But next day came, and gradually the storm abated. Though we had lost touch with our escort and our neighbor ships, another dawn found us standing off the harbor of our destination. Troops swarmed to the rails. While the sun pushed its red crown over the edge of the horizon, showing us the sight we were starved for, land, the Australian harbor pilot pulled alongside and climbed aboard in his long trench coat and dark felt hat.

In port in the bright morning we anchored beside the big ship that had been our portside neighbor all through the voyage. She had passed through the storm and reached the goal before us, and the soldiers who lined her decks yelled mocking greetings: "Hello, there, also-ran! Get the lead out of your pants!"

Ensign Fearless Parks went into the tourist business. He informed us that hotel accommodations ashore would be a cinch, a breeze. He then threw his signal crew into action and signaled from ship to town for fourteen rooms, with bath, at the best hotel.

"You're in, fellows," said Ensign Parks.

Unhappily, nobody caught the ensign's message. The best hotel was full to the roof, as it turned out, and we spent our first night in Australia in a hostelry conducted by the state temperance union—and no smoking in the dining-room.

IV

All Ashore

THE sun burned baldly on a strange city as the correspondents and cameramen commandeered an Army truck and rattled away from the docks on the left-hand side of the street—well in advance of the land-hungry troops, who had to await debarkation orders, and well in advance, sad to say, of Sergeant B., whose name I withhold in deference to his feelings.

Sergeant B. was fortune's plaything. He was the victim of one of those journalistic brainstorms that in past times have caused Presidents to pose unhappily for pictures in cowboy or Indian costume, and beautiful girls to illustrate the spirit of the cod-fish canning industry for the camera.

In brief, Sergeant B. was to be "the first American soldier to land from the convoy." There has to be a "first American soldier to land from the convoy," just as there has to be a mayor or deputy sheriff or ward-heeler to throw out the first ball at the start of the baseball season, with his arm cocked weakly in front of the lenses.

"Do you think we have to go through with it?" said the *Life* photographer, when we convened at sea beforehand to discuss the matter. You can see that this fellow was a bit of a left-winger, a downright iconoclast, in his line.

"Damn right we do," said the Associated Press photographer, a Tory, a man with a sense of tradition and principle.

So we combed the ship for the right "first soldier," and came up with Sergeant B. He was a World War veteran, he came from what the boys decided was a "key state," and he looked good. What's more, he had two nephews in his outfit, also sergeants.

Sergeant B. was reluctant at first, but nobody argues long with cameramen. We rehearsed the unfortunate fellow. We held him at bay for an hour-and-a-half, extracting his autobiography. We finally worked him into the spirit of the thing, and even had him looking forward to the moment when he, rifle in hand, with all the trimmings from immaculate overseas cap to white leggings, would set his foot proudly on Australian soil at the head of a file of his bold Yankee comrades from across the ocean—with cameras clicking right, left, and forward, two nephew sergeants marching just behind him, and the Australian public yelling greetings and waving handkerchiefs as it lined the streets to watch.

As it happened, the troops debarked at night. There

was no parade and no fanfare. We didn't meet Sergeant B. again, and, to be strictly truthful, some of us would have ducked around the corner if we'd seen him coming. We felt a little embarrassed toward the Sarge. After all, he never asked for the fame that the boys had arranged to confer upon his honest head.

If Sergeant B. was mortified when we struck Australia—and I doubt if he was, being a philosophical soldier, well used to the pranks of fate—the Commanding Officer and his staff were hopping mad. Their choler had nothing to do with sergeants or reception committees. They were angered by one of those foolish violations of common sense that sometimes occurred in the English-language press, both American and British, in the earlier days of the war.

While we were still a full day and night from port, a British newspaper carried a story which reached us at sea by radio—of a "gigantic convoy," even now "steaming through the Southwest Pacific toward Australia."

Publication of this spicy item caught us just entering the most dangerous stretch of water on our voyage. We knew little then of the whereabouts or disposition of Jap planes and submarines, but if any such characters were in action in our neighborhood—well, they had radios too.

The general, with his mind on the shiploads of

troops he was shepherding to their theater of operations, still crackled faintly with indignation when we
left the ships, safe in harbor, and moved into the town.
So did the rest of us who had seen or heard of the pre-
mature report. The fact that we forgot the whole thing
almost instantly on setting foot in Australia was a
tribute to the speed with which the ups and down and
blacks and whites of the kaleidoscopic wartime life suc-
ceed each other.

Also, it was a tribute to the strange new land that
lay before us in all its infinite variety. We had come a
long way to reach Australia—had been a long time
without seeing land at all. This was the place where
these troops of ours had been assigned by destiny and
their leaders to meet war. It was a land known only
by name, to all but a few. Maybe some of us expected
to see kangaroos lurching up the streets. We didn't, but
the American soldier can make these simple readjust-
ments in stride, and he proceeded to investigate and be
investigated.

Australia is worth investigating. Her people are
worth knowing and fighting side by side with, especially when the fight—as clear-thinking Australians lost
no time in telling us—was our own.

There can hardly be people in the world more
fiercely and fanatically independent than Australians.
The notion that the Yanks had come to "save" Aus-

tralia—well, some of us had it, sure enough, and there was no quicker way of tasting the quick mettle and genial scorn of the fellow we came to "save."

Today the Army guidebook recalls one of the incidents we witnessed in a bar in Sydney, in the first days of our intercourse with this free and easy ally. It was the incident of the American soldier who opened diplomatic relations with the Digger drinking shandy on his left by saying, "Well, boy, you can relax now. We're here to save you."

" 'Ow, is that it?" said the Australian, peering calmly into his glass. "I thought you were a fugitive from Pearl Harbor."

Down in Adelaide later, when a few of us were haunting the airline office night and day in search of transportation north to Darwin, I noticed a hostility in the girl ticket agent that could hardly be explained by the fact that we needed haircuts. I tacked around the subject before asking her point-blank what the trouble was, and she was mockingly courteous for some time—good stuff it was, too—before answering.

"Why, you all think you've come here to protect us," she said finally. "You're saving Australia all over the place. Of all the smug . . ."

I don't know how much her attitude was a matter of preconceived opinion, of reading her expectations into what she saw, of independence going more than halfway to defend itself, and how much it was actually bolstered by fact. At any rate, we learned that you don't save Australians any more than you save blue-jays. They are not the type.

Once he is sure you do not plan to save him, the average Australian—if there is such a thing—becomes hospitable practically to the point of adoption. I asked a pedestrian in Melbourne the whereabouts of a certain obscure street.

"I'll show you," he said, and started to walk away. When I stood still, puzzled by this maneuver, he looked over his shoulder and said, "Come on, I'll show you. It's only eight blocks and around a little corner."

As for the spiritual kinship between these two great peoples: I remember the time when I was joined by an elderly little citizen, of very respectable appearance, as I shuffled along an Australian city sidewalk. With his sober business clothes, bowler hat, and stylish furled umbrella, he looked like a banker, lawyer, or head of a small but well-to-do house of business. And no doubt he was one of the three.

"Have you heard that all tramcar and taxicab traffic will stop tomorrow in this city?" he said, falling into step with me and looking earnestly at my uniform.

The news startled me somewhat, and frankly I did not believe it, but I thought a gentleman so kindly and respectable in appearance as this one deserved an answer.

"Is that so?" I said.

"Yes. It will stop to take on passengers and also to let them off," said my informant, and with these words he darted away across the street, chuckling delightedly to himself and tapping the pavement with his umbrella.

Hell, I heard that one in Tampa, Fla., in 1937. Such is the brotherhood of man.

V

The Shirtsleeve Baedeker
(WARTIME EDITION)

THIS might be called *A Handy Guide to Australia and Propinquent Seas & Islands, Trespassing Somewhat on Standard Works of Reference, Highly Redundant, but Meaning no Offense & Hoping None is Taken.*

Or it might just be called *Highly Redundant in Australia,* a sequel to the author's earlier efforts in the field, such as *Highly Redundant on the Mississippi, Highly Redundant with Grant at Richmond, Highly Redundant on the Ocean's Floor,* and the *Return of Highly Redundant.*

The trespass is great, and the spirit of the guide is humble. When Benny, a semi-retired bookmaker with a keen interest in what goes on everywhere, asks me about bookmaking and parimutuel payoffs in Australia, and which way the horses run, I can tell him. When he asks me how many sheep there are in Australia per human being, I have to look it up or tell him from hearsay.

The point is, though, that Benny asks about both matters, and many others besides. So do soldiers, bartenders, cabdrivers, and athletes, and wives, mothers, and children, including my own. There is a lively, catholic interest among us in things Australian since we sent our first troops and our best-known military leader there. It seems to be a personal interest, of a kind that sheers away from textbooks and atlases and seeks for personal answers; much the same answers I sought myself.

My only regret is that I didn't get around to many dinner tables. A lady named Mrs. Thomas Anthony Trollope wrote a book about America based on our methods of picking our teeth in 1832 (what she wrote about us shouldn't happen to a dog). This is undoubtedly a surefire short cut to the understanding of any national culture, but I missed it, and all I can say is, that at an officer's table in Papua the bully beef was passable but the bread pudding only fair.

Answering that question of Benny the bookmaker's:

Q. How many sheep are there per person in Australia?

A. Seventeen.

And now, Mr. Baedeker, let us take off our coats and ties and proceed to business.

AUSTRALIA: The country is almost as big as the United States. If you see its east coast first, you get the

impression that it is very good country physically, for
the landscape is rich, green, and cultivated. From Brisbane north the weather is warm the year around, and
Darwin, Cape York, and northern Queensland are tropical. In the South, which corresponds to our North,
they have winter—in June, July, August, and September—but it is mild winter, chilly and damp sometimes
but seldom freezing. Australians talk about the weather
89 percent as much as we do. Cabdrivers are leaders in
this field.

When you leave the east and southeast coasts, you
find that Australia is really not good country physically, but old and worn out. There are broad stretches
of plain with enough water for cattle and all those
sheep to graze, but the center of the country is wasteland; thousands of square miles of nothing but what is
called Never Never Land, or a more forceful, unprintable name, by the Australians.

If you fly along the country's axis from Adelaide in
the south to Darwin in the north, you are bewildered
by the scope of the red waste of rock, ridge, and desert.
The map shows lakes, but most of them are salt pans
and nearly always dry.

You stop at desert towns like Oodnadatta, where the
flies are thick, and Alice Springs, where they settle on
your face in gangs, and Daly Waters, where they almost carry you off. A little one-track, narrow-gauge

railway runs along this axis some of the distance, the only inland railway in Australia. Where the railway has not been completed there is a highway of sorts, for road convoys. This is Darwin's sole supply route, except by air.

The little Toonerville train that travels cross-continent is worth seeing. I watched it scoot out of Darwin once just before an air-raid alarm. It had the look of one of those human Walt Disney trains, and you half expected the locomotive to duck into the bush beside the track for cover when Jap planes came overhead.

In the southwest of Australia there is a fertile corner, containing a fine town, Perth, with the handsomest girls in Australia. In the northwest there are a few pearling villages like Broome, Derby, and Wyndham, which the Japs have struck by air. In the thinly-peopled western country the only means of communication is a device called the pedal wireless, in which the power to transmit messages is generated by foot.

Australia's main railroad line merely follows the coast south from Queensland and around westward to Perth. There are five distinct gauges of railway on this route, and the problem of fast transport in bulk is a whopper; a problem which the five states gave little thought to when they built the railroad independently and piecemeal.

Piecemeal or not, the railway passes through some fine cities and fine country.

CITIES: Brisbane is a friendly, breezy frontier town. Adelaide is quiet, pretty, and conventional. Between them come Australia's two greatest cities, Melbourne and Sydney, which accommodate one-third of the country's entire population. I do not think the citizens of either place would dispute me if I said that there is rivalry between them, a rivalry felt more keenly by Melbourne, perhaps, as the slightly smaller, slightly younger, and slightly more cohesive of the two.

Sydney is Australia's "big town" in the sense that travelers apply the term to New York, San Francisco, and New Orleans. It is cosmopolitan and lively and a trifle cavalier in its relations with Melbourne. The latter, less a city and more a community, does however possess certain cardinal points of leadership. It is the sports capital of a sporting nation, especially where racing and football are concerned.

Melbourne has the world's happiest traffic cop. She also has dozens of Chinese restaurants, where you can obtain the local substitute for the hamburger, to "take out"—i.e., the *dim sim,* a ball of chopped meat spiced and wrapped in cabbage leaves.

NATIVES: Meaning the true natives, the Aboriginals or Abos, of whom there are some seventy thousand living in the bush country of Australia, the regions known as "Outback." Black and primitive, the Abos exist today in a state far more backward than that in which the white settlers found the Indians of North America.

The women are called *lubras* or Marys. Male and female alike, the Abos who have brushed against white civilization will risk their souls for tobacco. Most of the Abos I saw were in the Darwin region. They did some manual labor there, before the Jap bombings and the town's evacuation, and served as trackers and guides through the jungle country.

In the great Japanese bombing of Darwin on February 19, 1942, the town's jail was thrown open. Two of the inmates, serving terms for slight cases of murder, were Abo chieftains, Bullblow and M'Gilah, who had sworn to have each other's livers for breakfast if the opportunity presented itself. Big doings were expected when the two chiefs met in front of the jail, but the witnesses who lingered in the bombed town just to watch were deeply disappointed.

Surveying each other for about one-tenth of a second, the two chiefs made off in opposite directions and were eighty miles apart in no time. They seemed to feel that there was a time for fracturing the Sixth Commandment and a time for getting out of town.

A white citizen named Doyle, living with three lubras in the bush near Darwin, did good laundry work, though handling nothing but the executive end of the business himself.

WARTIME: War has brought sharper rationing to Australia than anything we have seen—of motor fuel, tobacco, liquor, cloth, tea, some kinds of food.

Australian cigarettes do not caress the American throat, but American cigarettes are impossible to buy —unless you are in or working with the American armed forces—and smokes of any kind are scarce.

The highways between cities are almost empty of traffic, except Army traffic. Our drivers managed to adjust themselves pretty quickly to the left-hand side of the street, though tending to shave the curb too closely and imperil the toes of pedestrians. This is balanced by the peril to American soldiers crossing streets, who always look the wrong way and do not perceive the omnibus rushing up from the blind, or right, side till its breath is hot on their necks.

Australian taxicabs today look like marvels of medieval alchemy, with big carbon-burning gadgets, masses of spouts and tubing, mounted aft or port or starboard to save petrol. That is, the cabs look like marvels of medieval alchemy if you happen to see one. If you happen to see an empty one at night, it is a marvel of chance, and sixteen people will rush out from a nearby ambush and grab it before you can reach it.

Cloth is so short that Australia long since stopped

making double-breasted suits and putting cuffs on trousers. There was a "clothing rush" in Melbourne the morning I set out to replace clothes I had lost on a trip to New Guinea. The rush was over by 10 A.M. and the department stores were reeling from the blows of the locust. At the third store I tried, I found "the last pair of drawers in town." They fitted all right.

In the first days of liquor rationing, some of the cities broke out in a small rash of "sly grog shops" (speakeasies). Who steered you to where the "sly grog" was? Correct. Cabdrivers.

DRINK: Beer is Australia's favorite potion, in war or peace. The best Australian beer is strong, and most Australians serve it and drink it warm. The line of Diggers waiting for a fresh beer ration at a camp in the jungle where I spent a few nights was as long and tense as a queue of American women waiting in front of a theater to see Tyrone Power in Person.

Shandy is a pretty good drink—ale with lemonade in it. Scotch whisky is hard to get now, and what is served in hotels has usually been cut. Rye and bourbon are virtually unknown; Australia's bad luck, you would say, if you tasted the sweetish "Australian whisky" which is made there but understandably is not much drunk.

VICTUALS: The country is pretty largely on meat-and-potatoes. The best vegetable dish, grown and served profusely, is asparagus tips, which even appear regularly in sandwiches.

Tea is the safest bet for a drink with meals, though it is strictly rationed now. Order coffee and you'll be asked "White coffee or black?" White coffee is stuff that comes to you full of milk. Order coffee in any form and you do so at your own risk.

Pork is hard to come by in Australia. There is plenty of beef, mutton, and lamb, and in most homes and in some restaurants it is well cooked.

RANDOM TIP: Soda fountains are called milk bars. You get a pretty good soda in a milk bar on Queen Street in Brisbane. I wish I could remember the address, but, anyway, if you look up the hotel run by the Queensland anti-alcohol league, the place I mean is right there in the same building.

SHARKS: Sharks occasionally bob up in the society notes as having participated in the bathing at certain fashionable beaches. Those are sharky waters off the east coast of Australia. In the Brisbane River I saw shark compounds—little squares of water palisaded off from the rest of the river for swimming and diving.

GIRLS: The girls of Australia are fine, handsome, fresh in the best sense of the word, and intelligent. Well, nearly all of them are intelligent. I observed one exception, who hoped that the war would be over by November so there could be a good field of horses and a properly gay spirit for the Melbourne Cup.

Being sports-minded to a degree beyond the power of American women, most Australian girls are willing to take the Melbourne Cup—and racing wherever they find it—without trimmings. Being intelligent, they are willing to take the war without the Melbourne Cup; though that is a far bigger order to Australians, feeling as they do, than war without a World Series would be to Americans.

Australian girls have sunny tempers and marvelous legs, strong and durable; which is all for the best, the taxicab situation being what it is.

ENTERTAINMENT: Some radio stations are operated by the government, some privately, all supplying a rough approximation of American radio fare. Competent critics tell me that the music and variety on the private stations is better than the government stuff. I didn't have much chance to listen.

Most of the motion pictures are American-made, which is to say, Hollywood. I called Australian girls intelligent just now, and intelligent they are, and beautiful too, but I am forced to report that one of the liveliest stirs of the war was caused by the rumor that Jimmy Stewart had arrived in Australia with the U. S. Army. All women are nuts to some extent.

N.B. In Australia, the expression is not "nuts" but "crackers."

It's a certain truth that much of what Australians

knew of our manners, customs and speech before our troops came in large numbers was gleaned from the movies. Is that a good thing? Well, one double feature I saw in Townsville, Queensland, consisted of *Ellery Queen's Penthouse Mystery* and Alice Faye and Jack Oakie in *The Great American Broadcast*. If you have to see those pictures to know what America is like, ignorance is best.

That show was exciting, though, as it happened. Townsville, a city alert for Japanese attack at the time, had an alarm as we sat in the balcony, with cigarette ends twinkling around us, and we strained to hear the sound of planes while Oakie invented the radio industry down there on the screen below. No planes came that day. Two Jap reconnaissance ships soared high overhead the next day, the first of the war to fly as far south as Townsville.

EPIDEMIC: Americans, a lot of them, have heard of the song *Waltzing Matilda*—a good, colloquial Australian ballad that was sung by the first Diggers to garrison Singapore in 1941. Having learned the tune from Dick Watts, New York dramatic critic and traveler, before I went to Australia, I thought I'd mastered the hit song of the war down yonder. As it turned out, *Waltzing Matilda* was widely known and highly esteemed among Australians, but *Bless 'Em All* was an epidemic.

BIG NIGHT: Australia's night out, her Saturday-Night-American-Plan, comes on Friday night. By Saturday evening her basically pious population of English-Scotch-Irish stock is beginning to taper off to a grave and immaculate Sunday that falls with an almost mortuary hush upon the ears of American soldiers stationed near towns and cities there.

That was one of the problems confronted by American troops with weekend or Sunday leave—the fact that practically everything, including motion picture theaters, was shut down tight as a snare drum on Sunday.

CASKET: Some parts of Australia have government lotteries, which was the way my shipmate of the voyage down, Private Bert Lynch, came to grief; I mentioned before how Private Lynch, announced as the winner of 6,000 pounds or $19,200, was checked at the gates of heaven by a ticket agent's discovery that he had mixed his initial with that of Corporal Dan Lynch, Australian, holder of the winning ticket.

The agent was a Golden Casket Agent. As you walk along the busy streets of, say, Brisbane, you will see shop after shop advertising "Casket Agency" and "Get Your Lucky Casket Here," and this is not the grim traffic of death but the merry traffic of get-rich-quick, taking its name from the gilded coffer from which the winning numbers are drawn.

Since I left Australia two more Yank soldiers have

sued a Digger for what they contend was their equity in a winning ticket he held. There is never a dull moment in the casket dodge.

RACING: Though tennis and football and cricket and sea bathing (called surfing) are pastimes pursued with fervent zeal by this daffiest of all sports-daffy nations, the racehorse is monarch of every Australian he surveys, and of every Australian's purse. It's no secret that the racehorse comes of a breed that grows more fickle the more you improve it. The horses I bet on galloped gently around the outside of the track, waving to friends in the crowd. Sometimes they even galloped clockwise, a British practice followed in Sydney and certain other parts of Australia.

Australia's wartime racing, however, is not wholly representative. It is confined to Saturdays. Some tracks —every crossroads, village, and city has one or more— are now army camps. The result is that all the horses in action at one track are funneled into a program of ten, twelve, or fifteen races once a week, with an average of close to twenty horses in a race. The further result is ruin for the man, woman, or child who bets on form.

There is parimutuel betting—Australia is the birthplace of the totalizator—and bookmaking as well. Australian bookmakers have no equals in the world in the magnificence of their checked suits, waistcoats, caps

or bowlers, and natty cravats. They are equaled elsewhere—but not surpassed—in the villainous lowness of
their odds.

There is no such thing as show betting, or betting
for third place, with either books or mutuels. You can
bet win and place, and place covers a horse finishing
either second or third.

I wish to acknowledge the courtesy of Mr. Cyril
White, of Melbourne, who paid off at 10 to 1 on the
only bet I won in Australia, and to Mr. Alf Wilson
of the same city who owned the next parasol in the
bookmakers' ring and said, "You been 'ad, Yank. I
would've given 12's."

PHAR LAP: There are one or two articles of faith
among Australian sportsmen that the Yank should be
warned against challenging. One is that Phar Lap,
the great Anzac racehorse, was poisoned to death in
America by an assassin's hand. Phar Lap died suddenly
just after winning first money of $50,000 in the Agua
Caliente Handicap in his only North American race.
If you think it was death from natural causes, do not
open your trap to this effect between latitudes 10 and
50 south and longitudes 110 and 180 east, embracing
New Zealand, where the mighty steed was bred, and
Australia, where the martyr's great heart is enshrined
in a museum.

There is also the case of a brilliant young Australian middleweight boxer named Les Darcy, who died in Memphis, Tennessee, of "mental breakdown and fever." The quotation marks are Australia's, and if you think they indicate suspicion, you are right.

INFILTRATION: We learned a grim lesson in the United States when the Japanese proved to have a better working knowledge of some of our fogbound Aleutian Islands than we did. Australia swallowed a dose just as bitter, when war came to the Pacific. She swiftly realized that Jap fishermen, who had plied the pearling ports of Darwin, Broome, and Wyndham, were in a position to chart those regions far better than she could. The same is true, Australian seamen told me, of the Great Barrier Reef, lovely, intricate wall of coral that fences Australia's northeast coast. If the Reef can be penetrated at all, the Japs are the ones who know how to do it.

ANIMAL LIFE: The koala bear has absolutely no lice or fleas, and eats several different kinds of eucalyptus leaf. The kangaroos, wallabys, and duck-billed platypuses are as advertised.*

CONCLUSION OF HANDY GUIDE: If the guide seems to wallow in trivia, and to emulate the capers of the jumping bean of Mexico, remember that Australia is 2,400 miles by 2,000, that it is infinite and various and alive with the juices of a strong and com-

* Note 2, page 292.

plex civilization, that I saw in it mainly what soldiers from abroad might see and what their friends and families at home might like to know about it.

It is a vast place and a human place. It is worth knowing better. In the months I spent there and on the seas and islands near there, my chief purpose was to watch and report the progress and background of war; but a man must be thick-shelled indeed who can fail, in that time, to savor the spirit which is Australia and which gives breath and a living pattern to his scrambled observations.

SUMMATION: May it please the court, it's a fine country.

VI

The Last Bastion

IN the late winter weeks of 1942, Australia was seeing her first Yank soldiers; at the same time, she was
wiping blood from her mouth. Japanese bomber planes
struck the port of Darwin on February 19, a date that
the townsfolk and soldiers who lived there will never
forget. Unopposed by air, lounging over their targets,
calling their shots, at will. A stray bomb along the
shoreline killed eight people in one house, including
the postmaster. The civilian hospital was hit in a separate raid that bombed and strafed the airdrome.

Within a short time Broome, Wyndham, and Derby,
little northwest Australia coast towns, were bombed.
Java fell, and back from this tragic, abortive battlefield straggled the survivors: Dutch and Australian
and British refugees, some en route from the earlier
disaster of Singapore; Dutch sailors and fliers, many of
them wounded; American airmen still cursing softly at
the memory of their planes destroyed on the ground.

Troops arriving fresh from America found the
thought of invasion in the air; frank fear of invasion

on the part of government leaders, who knew how
thin were Australia's resources to meet a full-dress attack by a foe prepared for the job. Whatever the Japanese plans were at the time, invasion seemed likely
to Australians and Americans.

"Australia is America's last bastion between America
and Japan," said Prime Minister John Curtin, calling
for more help for Australia's smooth but limited war
production, more help in manpower. The A.I.F., the
Australian Imperial Forces, not a large army at best,
were still in the Middle East. Sixteen thousand Australian soldiers had been lost in Malaya.

At Lennon's Hotel in Brisbane some of us sat
drinking beer with a Texas bomber pilot, Captain
Alvin Mueller. Mueller was busy running refugees out
of the doomed island of Timor, just south of the Indies.
He would land and take off by night on a strip of beach,
under the noses of the Japanese occupying force. It
was sleepless work.

"Know anything to keep me awake at the stick,
Doc?" he asked an officer of the Medical Corps.

The doctor wrote out a prescription for benzedrine.

Over the short wave radio came the voice of the
Tokyo spokesman of the evening. He was playing on
Allied apprehensions, and he was well informed.

"There are American officers and correspondents in

Lennon's Hotel in Brisbane," he said once. "We will come over and bomb them."

Mueller grinned, running his hand through his lank blond hair. He knew the Japs at first hand and they held no imaginary fears for him. He had won the *D.F.C.* at Christmas time, over Davao in the Philippines, when his Flying Fortress bombed Jap shipping in the harbor, guided the damaged flight leader home, and landed safely with more than a hundred bullet holes in her fuselage.

Another flier had just returned from a trip to Broome with medical supplies for that wounded little pearling port. He was young and emotionally shocked by what he had seen.

"They strafed the place," he said. "I saw one big Dutchman digging graves to bury his whole family. His wife and six kids. They got that far from Java, but then the Japs came over to strafe, and got 'em just as they landed in Broome. He dug the graves himself and buried his whole family."

It was easy to spot the Dutchmen in Australia, big fellows, nearly all of them, and nearly all bearded. One of them, a Navy officer, had had four vessels shot from under him in the brief flaring sea war in the Indies. He was wounded in the groin, and hobbled back to the hospital ship every night.

"I will leave there Tuesday and go to work again," he said.

"What does the doctor say?" a companion asked him.

"I'm bigger than he is," said the wounded man bravely, stroking his spade beard.

As for the Aussies and Yanks, there was no peril close enough, and no war talk grim enough, to blunt their mutual curiosity; I doubt if anything this side of hell could divert the unabashed, probing, ribald, friendly interest of the Aussie in a strange object. The Yanks on leave strolled along the sunny streets of Brisbane, a town that looks like St. Petersburg, Florida, suddenly galvanized into life. They peered into store windows, and when they paused, Australians came up and asked them questions: "How do you like Austreyelia, Yank? What part of the States do you come from? What's the weather like at home now, Yank?"

The country's strength was well mobilized. The only Australians we saw in the streets were women, old men, and soldiers.

At the hotel the ancient chambermaid refused a tip when I checked out, though she looked as if she could use it.

"I don't want your money," she said. "You people are here to help us."

This, however, was a temperance hotel that exercised its principles firmly, and gratitude did not extend to infringers of the three rules of the house. A young Naval officer splintered all three rules simultaneously. He landed in the street, followed closely by his luggage.

One day we boarded a train south. It was Australia's main railroad line, meandering along the coast through the country's handsomest landscape, with a different rail gauge for each State. Before we had been aboard twenty minutes, Australian Diggers—of an army labor outfit—were swarming over us, perched on the arms of our seats, hugging their knees on the floor of the aisle, asking questions, comparing dollar bills with ten-shilling notes, cheerfully offering the hospitality of the bottle and even more cheerfully receiving it.

"How do you like 'er, Yank?" said the corporal next to me. He extended a snapshot in a billfold, carefully holding it over the shoes of the Digger in the seat opposite, who had parked his large feet and bare legs in the corporal's lap.

It was a picture of the corporal's girl. It circulated among us, followed by a picture of the corporal's mother, the corporal's two sisters, the corporal's young brother and the corporal himself in a bathing suit.

"That's me, surfing," said the corporal.

From the seat opposite, two more Diggers started their own snapshots in motion, and pretty soon the car was a sea of photographs and battered billfolds passing from hand to hand. Presently a soldier stuck his head in at the door at the end of the car and yelled "Up, you bloody buggers!"

"The Mijor wants us," said the corporal, rising.

"I'll kick his rump," said the private beside him in the aisle, and cheerfully they filed away, the corporal turning to call over his shoulder, "Write me in Canberra, Yank, care of the prime minister. 'E does what 'e can for my pals!"

I have never seen an Australian train in a hurry. This mainliner loitered down the coast without a care in the world, though the three cars behind the locomotive were loaded to the gunwales with prisoners—internes, that is—of Italian birth. At a station down the line we saw the Italians stretching their legs on the platform, under guard. They seemed docile, except for one proud Roman who spat at the guards at regular intervals, haughtily but precisely.

An Australian sea pilot told me once, steaming along the Great Barrier Reef, that the fertile tropic stretches of northern Queensland off our port beam were thickly peopled by Italians, as many as 70,000, most of them sugar cane farmers. A British-Italian deal in the days of Garibaldi gave Italian emigrants easy access to Australia; they became the largest racial minority in the country, aside from the Aboriginals.

When war came, those of doubtful loyalty were interned. The sudden involuntary departure of the chef at Lennon's Hotel was actually mourned in certain circles in Brisbane—they tell me he was a mean hand with a skillet.

The train moved onward, to the best of its ability, towing us through the neat green fields of New South Wales toward Sydney. The locomotive was Casey Jones vintage. The Pullman car we rode in was said to be the oldest in Australia, built in the 1880's, with plain wooden berths, heavy print hangings over the doorways, curtains in the windows, and white enamel trimmings. There was no diner. At stations, occasionally, the soldiers piled out to buy tea and hot meat pies at the restaurant. By night we stopped at Coff's Harbor. A kid of about sixteen stuck his head in through the open window of the car. He just wanted to talk to Yanks.

"Three hundred men in our village enlisted in the army," he said. "That's near Coff's Harbor here, and it's more than 'alf our ablebodied men. I'll be in there next month if they don't remember 'ow I lied to 'em last month. Got a souvenir, Yank?"

A "souvenir" means an American coin; anything from a penny up is satisfactory.

Laying over in Sydney on a Saturday afternoon, I went to the races at Rosehill, where the horses proceeded clockwise—and reluctantly—over the drought-bitten turf. Men in uniform, American or Australian, are admitted free to the races. Once in, the American uniform wins you the hospitality of the track and its patrons. A Digger of Irish ancestry bought me a glass of shandy and told me he had three married sisters living in the Bronx. He then gave me Veiled Threat in the sixth race, and Veiled Threat came in breezing. I wasn't on it.

We came at last to the quiet and handsome city of Melbourne. The cab driver who took us from the station asked us for our names; what he was after was fresh evidence of America's mixed heritage, a constant source of wonder and entertainment to Australians.

"I drove three American soldiers yesterday," he said, struggling while he spoke to get action out of the weird charcoal-burner that perched in the rear of the cab like a laboratory on the half shell. "Three fine boys they were. There was one named Gonzales, one named, what was it, Thorgerson, and one named McNamara. They told me where their folks came from. This McNamara, he said he was half Scotch and half soda."

The cabby whooped with laughter. Apparently McNamara was a bit of a card.

Rationing was tight and getting tighter. A man was arrested the day I got to Melbourne with more than two thousand bootleg gasoline ration cards in his possession. They gave him four months in the brig and fined him a hundred pounds. There was a non-luxury campaign afoot with more than fifty variations, including the substitution of four-inch nails for coathangers. Old books and newspapers were pouring in for use in the manufacture of shell containers. This particular drive brought out, from the dark corners of Australian bookshelves and garrets, a staggering number of copies of that vermoulu British schoolboy classic "Eric; or, Little by Little," which must have warped more minds in its time than Tom Swift or Elsie Dinsmore.

For the American soldiers, who did not come to Australia loaded down with books, there was an acute reading shortage. In the camps near Melbourne the boys speedily evolved a gag about the private who went to a public library and, finding nothing else to take out, took out the assistant librarian.

I tagged along one day when Australian politicians and American and Australian army leaders inspected an American camp. For declamations and campaign speeches at the drop of a tent-flap, the Australian politician rivals the American Congressman. There was a speech every time two soldiers were careless enough to be found standing together, thus constituting a legal audience.

Colonel Geoffrey Galwey dropped out of the procession and peered into a vat of bubbling stew in front of the kitchen tent. Galwey, a painter and illustrator and now an American base commander, was an expert on stew.

"This is the same stew I used to make when I was on cook duty on the Mexican border in 1916," said the colonel, studying the contents of the vat, "or a very slight variation of the same stew. I was the envy of every cook on the border because my outfit held the local record for dysentery."

The men in the camp were among the first plain soldiers—land forces as opposed to airmen—to reach Australia. They hung about, anxious to talk to an American newspaperman. Private Bob Schulman, of Newark, New Jersey, wished to hear of the progress of Allie Stolz, lightweight fighter, since his manager, Hymie Caplin, went to jail. Allie, managed by remote control, is doing all right. Private Harry Penso, of the Bronx, whose racket at home, he said, was "hair stylist," told me that Johnny Mize would supply the punch the New York Giants needed.

"That short right-field wall will be Mize's dish," said Private Penso.

"How you getting on down here?"

"Oh, pretty good," said Private Schulman. "But I wish we'd see some action."

It was the airmen who were seeing the action in the Southwest Pacific. The pattern of the new war nearly always brings sailors and fliers into action first, and Melbourne was full of veterans of battle: slim young men in brown leather jackets, pilots, gunners, bombardiers, technicians, who had met Zeros and Mitsubishi bombers over the Philippines and the East Indies and Darwin and New Guinea, had bombed Jap shipping in the Macassar Straits, and had tasted the bitterness of failure in Java.

The Java defeat was a harsh and sour bellyful for youngsters fresh from American training fields and glorying in the fame and might of American arms. Java was littered with examples of the sharpest tragedy than can befall an air force: destruction of planes on the ground. It was a crimson case of too late and too little. I saw fliers who swore, bitterly and spontaneously, whenever Java was mentioned.

"With less than a hundred pursuit planes to help, we could have beaten them," they said.

I knew of one flight of pursuits that did reach Java from Australia—to be met at the coast, out of gas, at the end of their range, helpless, by a group of Japanese Zero planes informed somehow of their approach. The *P-40's* were nearly all shot down.

Lieutenant General George H. Brett told me more about Java. Brett, first American commander in Australia, dapper, drawling, and tough, saw the Indies' tragedy for himself. He spoke of the hasty, inadequate dispersal of such planes as we had on hand, of the rain and hub-deep mud that made landings and takeoffs doubly difficult, of the powerful—but, as it turned out, fruitless—bombing of the Japanese transports in the Macassar Straits; they still came on.

"Hell," said the general, "we'll get 'em soon. I learned in Java that we can outfly 'em."

Brett, the commander-in-chief till now, was about to turn over his command.

"My new boss is on the way," said the general.

"His new boss, coming by PT boat and plane from the rock of Corregidor in the Philippines, had set foot in Australia two days before.

VII

MacArthur and MacArthuriana

It was Saturday, March 21, 1942, just before ten
o'clock in the morning, when the Adelaide express
pulled into Melbourne station on track one, twenty-
seven minutes late, and General Douglas MacArthur
stepped onto the platform from a special car, the
second from the rear of the train.

It's hard to break the habits you form on Jacobs
Beach. Jacobs Beach is a stretch of asphalt in New
York City which constitutes the heart and vitals of the
prizefight industry. There the managers and handlers
and beachcombers and onlookers like myself have fallen into the way of saying "the big guy" or "the big
fella" in reference to the man who stands clearly at
the top, and alone—be it Joe Louis, pugilistically, or
Uncle Mike Jacobs himself, in the sordid financial
sense.

For a Jacobs Beacher there was no other way of
describing MacArthur as he figured in the eyes and
minds of the crowd that milled around the station that
day. When an Australian newspaper man standing on

tiptoe beside me on the platform said, "Is that he?"
pointing to an officer in the doorway of MacArthur's
car, I found myself replying, "No, the big guy ought to
be off in a minute."

The Australian gave me a quick startled glance before he turned his eyes hungrily back to the door of
the car. True, the general is not very large, as big men
go. But here and now he was "the big guy," to the
throng railed off from the platform, to the file of Philippine Scouts who stood at attention as guard of honor,
and to the cops, generals, aides, political dignitaries,
correspondents, and photographers who swarmed
tightly about the open semicircle before MacArthur's
car.

More than a record, military or otherwise, goes to
form this effect. There is facile but genuine magic in
such men. There is magic in MacArthur. I don't doubt
for a minute that the general knows it.

Not being a tickertape town, Melbourne contented
itself with flags that day. Its welcome had the jamboree
spirit of New York's reception of Gertrude Ederle or
the Atlantic-flyer-of-the-week, but in it too, of course,
were hope and exultation and common appreciation
of the facts of the hour: the enemy was sweeping all
before him, Australia and the whole Pacific were in
danger, and here from the Philippines had come the
one Allied leader with a record of skill and initiative

against the Jap. He had come by sea and air through the dangers of the ocean war. And he had a personal magic of word and manner.

"Get the hell back!" barked a colonel at a couple of correspondents edging to the front of the circle. He was a mild-mannered and pleasant man in normal circumstances, the colonel, but he was highly excited.

As the Adelaide express slid in, a dark, agile officer stepped from the general's car. It was Colonel Legrand H. "Pick" Diller, MacArthur's press officer at Corregidor, now to become chief censor for the United States Army in Australia. MacArthur's staff in the Philippines gave him his nickname, in arch but heavy reference to dill pickles. We had seen him a couple of nights before, when he slipped in to Melbourne for a quick look at the field and then slipped back to Adelaide to run interference for the general on the last lap of the long journey.

General Brett greeted him and walked aboard the train.

"This is it," said one cameraman to another.

The crowd, confined at the other end of the station, was too far away to see that this was it, but it held its breath on general principles and shuffled its feet.

MacArthur strode from his car. He wore a garrison cap and light khaki blouse and trousers. The khaki blouse was a victory for the press. Back home before we sailed for Australia, when we were buying our equipment, the list said "khaki blouse." We got them made to order for fourteen dollars apiece, and how the soldiers who sailed with us laughed—"Those things are for Washington soldiers. You won't see one of 'em abroad."

Okay, boys, take note that the general is wearing a khaki blouse.

MacArthur shook hands with all the Allied military leaders and statesmen in the reception queue. "How are you, Sir Charles, it's good to see you." He spotted Colonel Lloyd Lehrbas, a reporter in Washington when the general was chief of staff, and called "How are you, Larry, you old rogue?" They showed him the microphone, and he stood before it, suddenly tense, and unfolded a piece of paper. As he stood there reading, and I listened, I noticed that his dark, slightly silvered hair needed cutting.

The words he read were in his own handwriting, composed on the train the night before. They were a simple statement of faith and purpose, with now and then the odd turn of phrase and recherché figure or synonym that mark MacArthur's prose. It was moving to hear. Of course, you never can tell what a tabloid reporter will do. The general dwelt with high eloquence upon his closing sentence: "I will keep the soldier faith." There was deep silence, broken by Jack

Turcott, the over-strong banjo player from the *New York Daily News.*

"How's that, General?" said Jack.

The general met the anticlimax with dignity.

"I will keep the soldier faith," he repeated slowly, and Turcott, slightly carmine around the ears, made a note of the fact.

With General MacArthur in the car that brought him to Melbourne were his wife, his little son Arthur, named for the general's father, the Civil War soldier, and the boy's Chinese amah, a lady of ancient wisdom named Ah Chu. The general got into one automobile, as specified in the reception program. His family got into another. The cars rolled slowly between sidewalks black with cheering people, and the representatives of the *New York Times* and the magazine *Time* tore up the notes they had just made. The boys had been interviewing an Army chauffeur, with copious data on his school days and happy childhood, in the expectation that he would drive MacArthur's car. He didn't. It was the wrong chauffeur.

By the time we reached the hotel on foot, the single elevator in the lobby had swallowed up the MacArthur party. Crowds still pressed thickly about the entrance, to see what else might be seen. A policeman on the fringe of the throng paid homage to the general.

"Even the Collins Street Squatters turned out to see him," he said.

The highest tribute Collins Street Squatters—drug store cowboys—can pay is to travel a full long block from the scene of their spinal patrol. Collins Street is Melbourne's main street, and a fair, wide, and pleasant one too.

Weaving and bobbing through the lobby, I found MacArthur's staff engineer and fellow voyager from the Philippines, Brigadier General Hugh J. Casey, spare, dapper, trimly mustached—a Brooklyn boy who made good on Luzon, namesake of a Georgia boy who made good in Brooklyn, fat Hugh Casey, the Dodger pitcher. This young general was the father of Casey's Cookies, homemade grenades that blasted many a Jap emplacement. I'd heard that Casey, before Manila was left to the enemy, had destroyed more than $25,000,000 worth of property.

"How much did you actually destroy, General? What was the bill?"

"I don't know," said Casey, with the slightest of smiles, "but I'd hate to have to pay it."

Others of MacArthur's staff were herded into corners of the dark old lobby. Gradually we pieced together the story of the grim journey from Corregidor that began on March 11, eighteen days after President Roosevelt ordered the leader of the forces in the Philippines to leave his hard-pressed army and go to Australia to take command of the whole Southwest Pacific area.

You have heard how the expedition left the little island rock in the mouth of Manila Bay in PT boats, seventy-foot torpedo boats worn down to not much more than 30 knots of speed. You may not know how a PT boat rides, in even a moderate sea—it is outboard motorboating multiplied five times, as the craft rears on her tail and then slaps the water full force, again and again. Some of the men in the party were sick throughout the trip.

At a point in the south of the Philippines the expedition picked up two *B-17's,* Flying Fortresses, and flew two thousand miles south-southwest across Oceania to Darwin. In the Darwin region later, I talked with the officer who put the general aboard a fresh plane there on his way to Alice Springs, in the heart of Australia's "Gawd Helpus" country.

"I wanted to explain to him how we didn't have a plane that was fixed up very good, because I figured maybe he expected to ride comfortably, air line style," said the young dispatcher. "Hell, he never said a word. He just got in and took the seat we showed him and never said nothing. You know, abstracted."

After taking over the reins, MacArthur made a quick trip to Canberra, the national capital. There is seldom a dull moment in Canberra when parliament is in session. The general, sitting with knees crossed on a chair on the floor of the house, saw the boys go after each other without gloves. One plump representative was openly scornful of the speaker of the moment.

"Get this, Doug," he called over to the general. "This'll kill you."

"Say that again," he yelled a few minutes later. "I want Mac to hear this."

With or without formalities—and the average Australian prefers to do without—the country lionized Mac-Arthur from the start. Not that he submitted to much lionizing in the banquet and public-appearance sense; I doubt if a military headquarters was ever more strictly business or a hero harder to find.

At his hotel the general and his family and staff occupied an entire floor. Melbourne saw Mrs. MacArthur and young Arthur sometimes, shopping, going to the zoo, but almost never MacArthur himself. A lull followed Japan's decision to concentrate her forces in Asia after the conquest of Java and Burma. In the north of Australia and in New Guinea, under MacArthur's command, there was punishing, smashing air warfare, the warfare I was about to go and see for myself; the first real test of matched strength between Japan and the Allies. Then followed Japan's acknowledgment of the needle in her flank—her thrust with ships into the

Coral Sea, and her brutal beating there and her rout by planes.

There was a time, soon after the general reached Australia, when some newspaper men felt that his "position" was not "clear." The fact that reports to this effect were permitted to pass through MacArthur's censorship office to the United States was taken to mean that the general felt the same way. I don't know. Neither does anyone else but MacArthur. We had good reason to believe, however, that arrangements, then and later, were not too satisfactory to his "spokesmen."

I heard the general talk at length in a press conference soon after he set up his headquarters. Much later, with three companions on a tour of the northern air front, I heard him talk again in his office—an hour and a half of the most gripping disquisition on this and other wars that ever mesmerized a male quartette. These talks were off the record. I can only say, in the light of subsequent events, that the man called the shots.

There's one thing about MacArthur's conversation; you follow it with ease if you are an intelligent adult— i.e., a sports writer. Not only was the general a good ball player in his youth, but he knows the fight racket. When he drew upon the career of Jimmy Gardner to illustrate a point at his first press conference, I sensed a doltish ignorance among my colleagues, a spirit of "what the hell is he talking about?" The trouble with most of these fellows is that they are enslaved by world affairs. They lack the big, broad, flexible outlook.

As a matter of common mercy, I explained to six Americans and two Australians later, that Mr. Gardner was a Boston middleweight who hailed originally from Lisdoonvarna, County Clare, Ireland. He was a fine broth of a bye, as the general pointed out, and when speculation arose as to what had happened to one of his opponents in the ring—foul, stroke, dysentery, or what—James explained it simply: "I hit him."

The general also alluded to Willie Keeler, the old Baltimore Oriole and New York Highlander, for whose policy of "hit 'em where they ain't" he expressed great respect.

Within a few days of his arrival in Australia, there was a MacArthur Salad on the bill of fare of the Hotel Australia in Melbourne, which I did not probe, and at certain milk bars or soda fountains a MacArthur Sandwich, a doubledecker consisting, at the place where I caught the number—there may have been variations—of ham, lamb, and mayonnaise.

Even Babe Ruth never had a sandwich named for him, that I know of. The best the Babe could do was a candy bar.

VIII

Road Company

BECAUSE I was almost never out of sight or sound of them for the next twelve weeks and twelve thousand miles—because we bunked together in tents, huts, planes, hotels, trains, ships, and deserted houses, in nearly every city of Australia, in every crevice of the Australian war zone and every mile of smooth or sulky Pacific between Melbourne and the United States—I find it is going to be impossible to ignore my three traveling companions.

They were good to travel with. They were sanitary, scenic, and seldom dull. Their poker ranged from fair to "pleasing wild," as the ball players used to say of Bob Feller's fast ball. They were good listeners when absolutely necessary, and they were kind to animals as a general rule.

However, had they been dullards of the first water, I would still be driven by common courtesy and the thought of all the razor blades, carbon paper, and ten-pound notes they lent me to give a short account of these three characters:

Allen Raymond, a dreamer, from New England.

Hubert Renfro Knickerbocker, an eclectic, from Texas (eclectic: one who practices selection from all systems or sources, as in philosophy or medicine—*Funk and Wagnalls*).

Ralph B. Jordan, a practical man, from Utah by way of Hollywood.

The dreaming of Raymond was divided into two categories. His waking dreams were beautiful, idealistic, and visionary. It was a pleasure to hear him daydream. His sleeping dreams could also be heard, but I would not give a nickel for a 5 per cent share of any one of them. They were turgid and violent. Raymond asleep in a tent or on a boat was the closest thing to a full-dress performance of Wagner you could get on short notice.

Knickerbocker, red-haired and a man of wide tastes and attainments, had one flaw in his character. He was an exploiter at heart, a promoter of sordid tests or competitions for the betterment of his worldly estate. I little suspected, when he wagered me a round sum I couldn't do twenty push-ups from a fairly firm floor, that he would count three times over, each of the last five push-ups and practically kick my spine into the carpet to gain his ends.

Happily for society, this predatory fellow had a weakness. His poker was bad. He did beat me out of one of the largest pots (on paper) I ever played in, but when I learned that he had accomplished this feat by misreading my hand, I felt no compunction about taking the money back with a few skillful tosses of an Australian shilling.

Somewhere in Knickerbocker there must have been a good streak. I read him the *Book of Ecclesiastes* one evening from start to finish, and when it was over he was silent for ten minutes and then repaired to bed, looking almost like a decent citizen.

Jordan had a good heart, too, and the worst singing voice that ever came out of Utah. A college athlete on the Coast in his prime, he spent his later years investigating murder cases around Los Angeles—where they throw a murder back if it isn't grotesque enough, like killing your niece with fishhooks in a vat of prune juice —and studying life in Hollywood.

It is very handy to have a man along who knows the difference between Lana Turner and Veronica Lake.

And there, coming right down to it, is the first requirement for good companionship on the road: mutual contribution to the pool of knowledge. This unit was practically self-sufficient. There was Jordan to enlighten Raymond, who thought Veronica Lake was a pellucid sheet of water in the hills near Banff. There was Raymond to tell Jordan that the phrase "it stinks," far from being the invention of a Hollywood producer with a headache, traces directly back to Shakespeare.

Raymond was very handy with all the classics of literature, from Herodotus on. He was Dr. Eliot's five-foot shelf with the curse off, and knew the complete words of "Frankie and Johnny" and "Casey at the Bat" to boot.

Knickerbocker had the *Encyclopedia Britannica* by heart from *A* to *J* and *N* to *Z*. He had lost the two middle volumes in a crap game, and this sometimes created painful gaps in his conversation which he filled in by singing *Bless 'Em All*, the hit song of Australia, or a rousing number we picked up in New Zealand called *Maori Battalion, On to Victory*.

Jordan, besides Los Angeles homicides and the film industry, was an authority on track and field and horse-racing records since 1920.

As for me, the boys were welcome at all times to useful information on the treatment of snakebite, the superiority of the Algonquin Indians over the Iroquois, the Black Sox scandal, and the rules of red dog. They exercised this privilege very cautiously.

There was no Dan Beard among us—as a matter of fact, none of my roadmates could start a fire with a box of matches, let alone two dry sticks—but we had practical talents, just the same, suitable for life in the wilderness. Jordan was the best procurer of supplies I ever saw in action. We carried no guns, but Knickerbocker rendered us invulnerable to attack by land by borrowing a blackjack from one Major Thomas Taylor, former boxing commissioner and official of Kansas City. And when the vehicle we rode in Papua became stuck hub-deep in mud, the boys gave me the keenest and most valuable sort of advice on how to extricate it.

Raymond was a painter in his spare time. His impressionist study in water colors, *A Tree, not far from a Wall,* painted near Melbourne after our return from the front, reminded observers very strongly of Cézanne in his late period. And, remember, this was only Raymond's middle period. There seemed to be every likelihood that he would overhaul the Frenchman in the stretch.

My notes reveal that bets on the spelling and pronunciation of words—with *Webster's Collegiate Dictionary* as sole and final authority—resulted as follows: Knickerbocker, 7 wins; Raymond, 5 wins; Lardner, 4 wins; Jordan, 1 draw. Knickerbocker, by a series of curious coincidences, would introduce these bets after an hour of close communion with the dictionary.

Planning their lecture tours of the United States, Raymond and Knickerbocker apportioned the country between them by dealing cold poker hands. When they adjourned, Knickerbocker had South Bend, Indiana, and nothing else.

There were long spells of calm in our twelve-week journey, which will not figure in this record of the scenes and adventures of war. I'll fill the gaps in advance by saying that during such times the four of us argued (in some cases, more than once) the following themes:

Food; Russia; women; the Louis-Schmeling fights; the art of Michelangelo; the Civil War; religion; the Newspaper Guild; Cornelia Otis Skinner; tattooing; the best place to live in New England; William Randolph Hearst; war production; venereal disease; the Pyramids; walking-sticks; dining out as opposed to dining home; the private life of Hedy Lamarr; marriage; *For Whom the Bell Tolls;* prizefight managers; education for children; Enzo Fiermonte; Paris; this war and all others; Leopold and Loeb; San Francisco restaurants; Greek and Roman architecture; Seabiscuit; the comparative merits of Cleopatra and Mary Queen of Scots.

And several hundred others.

These fellows, as I said before, were good to travel with. In cities, they would order a cab to journey a block and a half, but in the bush and dusty jungle of the war zone, when the necessity arose, they would cheerfully bend their feet to the task of getting from one place to another. They were adaptable and understanding, and none of them, so far as I know, smoked hop or robbed birds' nests.

Above all, each man professed courteously to admire the writings of each of the others. As long as this stout convention held good—and it never tottered—the union was safe.

IX

Darwin

IT was after nightfall when the town, harbor, level swamps, and dark islands of Darwin appeared beneath our plane, with the Timor Sea and Van Diemen Gulf stretching grayly to the north. The Equator was only thirteen degrees away, but the night seemed cool after our flight across Australia and her angry red desert.

Suddenly, searchlights from the ground picked us up. They caught and rocked us in a cradle of light that flooded the interior of the ship. There must always be quick, sharp fear in the belly of the enemy flyer who is undressed in the air like this by the probing white shafts from below. It's tense enough in a friendly plane; until they know you're a friend.

Darwin was prepared for any visitation. The Japs, based on Koepang on the island of Timor, four hundred and fifty miles to the northwest, had been bombing and strafing her almost daily since the crimson hours of February 19, when the first raid blasted Darwin's port and served notice on Australia that its turn had come to taste fire.

That raid was perhaps the most onesided of the war, in South Pacific waters. By now, more than a month later, the pattern had changed. Australians and Americans had pursuit planes in the air. More than that, they were sending their own bombers over to cudgel Koepang and the shipping there. The fight had settled down to a match of the strengths and skills of our pursuits and the Jap Zeros, of our bombers and theirs. On the latter count, at least, we were forging ahead.

We landed, on a field puddled by recent tropic rains, to hear that the Japs had bombed Darwin that afternoon and totally eliminated a white leghorn chicken that was crossing the road—bound on the errand that is one of the great riddles of the ages. The chicken surrendered quietly. He constituted the casualty list for the day.

When Tojo came over again next day, he was looking for bigger game than poultry.

It was Good Friday. Toward noon Raymond and I, having bivouacked in the bush some miles south of Darwin proper, hitched a ride into town in an army command car. Our driver was Sergeant Bill Bailey, a slight, leathery, hatchet-faced artilleryman from Texas. He pumped the car along the "Burma Road" at a good clip.

This road was not Darwin's main, but her only, artery—combined with the narrow-gauge railway that

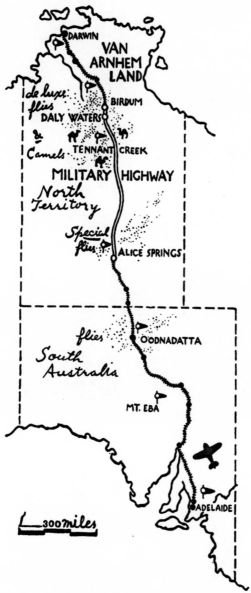

Route from Adelaide to Darwin

ran along beside it. With the town deserted, the road was the focus of traffic and human intercourse. It rambled for miles. Trucks, jeeps, cars, and wagons rattled north and south, kicking up clouds of red dust that filled your hair, mouth, and ears and sometimes reduced visibility to zero.

The white leghorn had been crossing the Burma Road the day before. It was Hobson's choice, and he took it.

We passed soldiers wallowing naked under showerbaths by the roadside. This was a womanless region. We passed one soldier, nearer town, who jerked his thumb toward the sky. He didn't seem to be hitchhiking. A few minutes later we passed another, an Australian, and he yelled at us and stabbed his finger upward with grim emphasis. At the same instant a siren began to wail.

"They must be up there," I said to Bailey.

The sergeant nodded briefly. He peered along the edge of the road for the hole he wanted, and suddenly swung the car into the brush, beneath the thin shelter of a gum tree. We piled out.

We could hear the zooming of planes now. It was a day of blistering heat, motionless green below and blue above, with a bank of fat white clouds almost straight above us. From somewhere among these clouds came the rattle of machine-gun fire. Then, suddenly, planes broke into view at a point that seemed directly over-head, little black *X's* stenciled against the brilliant blue sky.

The sight that followed was breathlessly beautiful from the point of view of an artist—and exhilarating, too, from ours. I saw many air raids later, but this was the sharpest and most theatrical presentment of death in the sky.

Along the edge of the cloudbank small white puffs of smoke appeared—anti-aircraft shells exploding. The sixth of these puffs was close to a plane, and the next moment, as though drawn magnetically into line, the Japanese bomber coincided with the gunner's aim and became an orange ball of fire. It hurtled to the ground —not on top of us, as we judged it would, but a good mile away. A piece of the plane, also in flames, flut-tered slowly and separately to earth like the soft burn-ing ruins of one of those fire balloons you see on the Fourth of July.

Off near the horizon two more Jap ships were losing altitude and trailing thick gray smoke.

When machine-gun fire suddenly spoke loud and clear above us, we dived under the car. Bailey's hand moved instinctively to the stock of his rifle. Then he smiled foolishly and turned sideways to see if I had noticed the movement. As he did so, grease from the entrails of the car smudged his cheek. The sergeant swore.

The raid lasted less than thirty minutes, and when it was over the armed camp of Darwin subsided into a sleek, happy glow to wait for the official score. This was still a new thing, the sight of Jap planes falling. Our anti-aircraft guns were new, and so was the disposition of our interceptor planes. We were learning. Till now the Japs had held control of the air.

"You don't know what a lousy feeling it is," said a soldier who emerged from cover by a log near by, "to see those bastards drop their loads and then go flying off in formation, flicking their tails at you. Today was really something. I got a kick right up from my shoes when I saw them fall. And it wasn't just the ack-ack either, boy. The P-40's got some of 'em. I wonder how they managed to get on top of those bums."

As it turned out, the raid was perfectly timed from the Allied standpoint, and for once our P-40's, our pursuit planes, got an opportunity that seldom came to them—the chance to attack the enemy from above. The P-40's had been on patrol, at a good height, at the moment the Jap bombers came over somewhat lower. When half of our planes went down to attack, the Zeros—those high-flying, razor-sharp enemy pursuit ships—followed, and the rest of the P-40's in turn descended upon the Zeros and routed them.

In short, it was one of those days, with the anti-aircraft gunners getting two and possibly three bombers with the first burst they fired: the burst we saw from below. When ground guns connect at heights like that, you know the Gods are with them.

I left the car at the head of Darwin's main street and walked in the blazing sun through the town I had heard so much about: a wild little tropic port cut off from the rest of Australia by vast sweeps of jungle and desert, a town with an evil and sinister name among the peaceful Australians far to the south; sullen, discontented, the refuge of beachcombers and aliens, and sometimes of gamblers and petty criminals. Once in the past, when the great Vestey's meat-packing house attempted to base in Darwin and built its plant there, a labor war broke out, so hot and fierce that the effort was never repeated. Today the Vestey's plant is a long, empty, haunted barrack, riding a little ridge just back of the town, near the "Toonerville" railroad yards.

It is hard for Americans to comprehend Darwin, from the map. The map shows it to be the only seaport in Australia's broad north coast; which argues, to the American mind, a city teeming with the traffic of land, sea, and air. We overlook the savage realities: the heat, rains, swamps, flies and mosquitoes of Darwin, and above all the untamed, unarable wilderness that blankets two-thirds of Australia and has thus far con-

fined her commerce to fertile corners in the southeast
and southwest of the continent.

By land, Darwin is hooked to civilization solely by
the little piecework railroad I spoke of and the dusty
desert highway that ekes out the railroad. By sea, in
peacetime, she was chiefly a pearling port, and the
Japanese in that trade knew her well.

The airways alone kept her name alive in the minds
of most Australians. She is the last jumpoff point for
Asia and Europe by air, the first landfall of planes
bound south. Kingsford-Smith and other pioneer Empire fliers made the dateline of Darwin familiar in the
newspapers. She became an air base of importance. But
in peacetime her unstable population never exceeded
4,000.

And now, when I found her in war, she was a ghost
town. Many chickens and a few soldiers scratched or
shuffled in her streets, though most of the soldiers,
Australian and American alike, had seen all they
wanted of the empty town itself by this time and remained to work and prepare for battle in their camps
in the neighboring bush. The Aboriginals had been
evacuated from the region soon after the port was
shattered and the town looted—by certain of its inmates—on February 19. Here and there you saw a griz-
zled Abo taking the sun in front of a deserted store;
more likely than not a tracker. There were times when

soldiers wandered optimistically into the bush to explore or to shoot at alligators with revolvers, and there were times when they got lost. Only the Abos could find their tracks in that country.

Walking up the main street, I heard a call from the shadows of a ramshackle shop across the way, and turned to see an ancient beachcomber in a battered straw hat step forward.

"You see the shooting today?" he said. "They can really shoot. Who was it, the Marines?"

"Nope. Regular anti-aircraft."

"That was bloody wonderful shooting," said the aged gentleman, picking his teeth. "I walked right out in the street to see it."

I asked him the whereabouts of a photographer's shop I'd heard about, whose Japanese owner had jumped town before the bombing and later turned out to be, according to local rumor, an officer in the Jap navy. He pointed out the shop. It was one of a row of low clapboard booths and buildings with their signboards still hanging over the doorways. These signboards told how cosmopolitan the flavor of the town had been.

Next door to the prim headquarters of Thomas Brown, Ltd., across the street, was the Soleres Kafcaloudes, sharing the building with P. H. Mendis, pearl merchant, and the Blue Bell Squash Shop. On

my corner stood the house where Sun Cheong Loong
had done business as tobacconist, patent-medicine
agent, draper, and outfitter. Hard by the Mura Photo-
graphic Studio, which somehow looked even emptier
than its neighbors, was Barney Chan's Oriental Café,
Pastry a Specialty, and beyond that was the American
Service Co. All kinds of *Hamburghers*. Farther along
the street a sign invited you to rent the auxiliary launch
Violet by day or hour. The Moonlight Café, late suppers, rubbed elbows with Man Fong Lau & Co., and
the crowning glory of the dusty Prado was Kyriakos'
Tropical Delicatessen and Cold Suppers—Zero in the
Tropics.

Down by the harbor was a cluster of buildings,
fronted by long, unsteady verandas, that formerly
housed the legal administrators and public servants of
Darwin. During our stay, some of us invaded the
judge's chambers and the courtroom, a ghostly courtroom littered with papers and files and stationery and
casebooks and records and briefs. In front of the jury-
box were six Bibles set neatly in single file down the
length of a table and coated with dust. The judge, the
last time he sat, had clearly been trying a case that
involved rival claims to a parcel of gold-bearing land
on one of the islands across the harbor. The papers
strewn across his desk and on the lawyers' tables spoke
of nothing else.

From the road in front of the courthouse we could see this island and others—one of them contained a leper colony.

Later, with an American colonel, we picked limes from the lime trees in the yard of the Australian Navy headquarters, now vacant, next door to the courthouse. Limes make ticklish picking, for the trees are thorny; but, as the colonel pointed out, limejuice was the only thing that could take the curse off the drinks he planned to make, from a type of Philippine gin almost completely without virtue.

It was on this same day that we explored the new hotel. The hotel represented a brave attempt to find "resort" possibilities in Darwin and to bring luxury service to airline passengers. It was a white building, low, and rambling, tropical in style; it looked handsome from a distance, but when we searched the barren catacombs within, we found the building was a shell, looted down to the nails in the walls. There were broken bottles on the floor of the central dining room, that once held beer, ale, and liqueurs. Upstairs in the bedrooms there was nothing but emptiness, except for one trophy I found in a dark corner of a clothes-closet: a ready-tied, "easy-duz-it" bow tie for evening wear, with a series of hooks in the back to accommodate any size of neck.

"How did they overlook that?" said an Australian

soldier who made the rounds with me. "It's the only thing left here that isn't nailed down."

The senseless looting that stripped Darwin on the day of her disaster shocked the Australian military leadership as much as it did the Americans stationed there. It represented the special character and temper of Darwin's population. It led to a mass flight with booty down the "Burma Road," in wagons and cars and even "ice cream bicycles" such as our Good Humor men use, all laden with loot. Most of the fugitives were rounded up and held at desert stations to the south, like Katherine, Daly Waters, and Adelaide River, since there was only one road they could follow.

An Australian officer, public librarian in Darwin before the bombing, told me how he rushed home from the library when the bombs started falling, to look after his wife and children, and returned to find hardly a book left. Weeks later we heard another echo of this strange day. A handful of sailors were arrested in Brisbane, charged with buying stolen property from looters when their cargo ship touched at Darwin just after the Japs struck. The stuff they had aboard included typewriters, sewing machines, and a kitchen stove.

Finally, on a leafy corner near the main street, we came upon the most grotesque spectacle the town had to offer. A little house stood there, surrounded by a yard and a wire fence. Two great emus lay in the yard, stiff and stark. The toes of these birds, which are ostrich-like and harmless and peculiarly Australian, pointed straight upwards. Nearby were some dead alligators and a few smaller birds, also dead. They had all been shot.

The house belonged to an old citizen of local notoriety who kept a pet shop and dabbled in espionage on the side. He had been arrested two days before. Told to dispose of the pets, the town's "constabulary" enthusiastically shot holes through the emus and alligators and whatever else they could not sell. One fine pink cockatoo escaped by the skin of his bill when an American captain happened by and bought him for a pound. The captain took the bird back to his tent, named him Joe, and made a pet of him.

"I know a little about these birds," he told us. "Joe is worth around $300. But not in Darwin."

Thus, the ghost town stood there at the topmost pole of the dusty road across Australia, brooding over its scars and its stigmas. And back in the bush, ignoring the town, the troops lay in wait, and overhead the planes fought the Jap raider or roared north to raid the Japs. Most Australians expected the enemy to move on Darwin first, if he invaded the country. The troops did not speculate much. They were there, and they were ready. The flyers, being at grips with the enemy, did not speculate at all. They fought, and learned as they fought.

It was a full, strange life that thrust itself upon our flyers down there in the crannies of the southern Pacific and the fringes of the Indies seas; something more than a matter of plane engines and technical performance. Each man was prepared to be Captain Cook or Robinson Crusoe or a castaway from the *Bounty* at a moment's notice. Take the case of Sanford: Lieutenant Clarence S. Sanford, from Auburn, New York, a young fellow just old enough to vote, who was saved from death at the business end of a spear by the crucifix he wore around his neck.

Your map shows you the Gulf of Carpentaria, a big gouge of water in Australia's north coast. Sanford's flight of pursuit planes took off from the Cape York region, met the Japanese over the gulf, and engaged them successfully—except that Sanford, as often happens in the whirls and dives of a dogfight, lost his bearings and his company. His fuel was low by now. He decided that the nearest land lay westward, and he headed that way.

He kept above the clouds, to get more mileage. When his gas ran out, Sanford dropped through the clouds to find how his luck stood. He saw land, about three miles ahead. He glided the plane as far as he could, bailed out, and somehow managed to swim to the shore, where he fainted from exhaustion.

When the young man from Auburn, New York, awoke, he found two Aboriginals standing beside him with their spears in their hands. They saw that his eyes were open, and promptly brought the points of their spears into juxtaposition with his chest.

"You Jap?" said one of the Abos.

This was a hypothesis that Sanford had never foreseen, and the faces of the two natives told him that unless it was corrected it promised poorly for him. He denied strenuously that he was a Jap. He tried to move into a less ticklish position, and his shirt fell open, revealing the cross around his neck. The Abos were instantly satisfied.

"That mean Christ, white number one Man," said the spokesman.

They fed Sanford and took him from the little island off wild Cape Arnhem to the nearest mission, five hundred miles away. There the pilot learned that his luck had been even better than he thought, for the natives came only once a month to the island where he landed, and without them he would never have reached civilization—which is to say, Nillimimbi and eventually Darwin.

War has taken men like Sanford a far piece from the country club and the corner drug store.

X

Japs, Mostly Dead

It is hard to tell the age of a Japanese when he is alive. It is no easier when he is dead. I saw a big fellow fished out of a fallen bomber in low beach water near Darwin who might have been anywhere from twenty-one to forty-five; a strong fellow, fat and broad, built like a wrestler and weighing more than two hundred pounds.

He was the pilot, with better clothes and equipment than the men in his crew of four. He had gloves, leather gauntlets, each stamped with two yellow Japanese characters. Near his body were the ruins of a pair of fleece-lined boots—blown off by the concussion of the shots that wrecked his plane, as often happens with boots, socks, and gloves. He had a heavy coat of good quality that may have been designed for export, since the label in Japanese lettering was superimposed upon the Japanese maker's original label in English.

The pilot wore a belt-of-a-thousand stitches, a luck-piece of a type found on many Jap flyers, made of heavy silk fabric elaborately embroidered. He carried no watch or money; nothing but a knife and a scrap of paper that seemed to be a cancelled bill.

Apart from his size, he was a representative specimen.

The men of his crew were dressed more cheaply, in coveralls of shoddy brown felt that were nonetheless lined with silk. They carried no valuables. None of them wore glasses. When the war began there was an article of America's credo which said that Japanese airmen were handicapped by the "national" weakness of Japanese eyes. If our own fliers ever shared this notion, they swiftly learned to take salt with it.

"They find their way around pretty good," Captain Jerome Tarter told me dryly. Tarter was a bomber pilot from Kentucky whose own pale blue eyes looked sharp enough to pierce an asbestos stage-drop.

Early in the war, and without great reluctance, Americans and Australians came to accept the truth that any Jap they laid their hands on was apt to be a dead Jap. Our enemy followed blindly the semidivine (and highly official) injunction not to be taken captive. He fought from caves in the Solomon Islands till he was blown up with his cave. In the Philippines he clung to his sniper's tree till bullets brought him down. He showed Americans his attitude toward death as early as January 4, 1942, in the first attack on our Abucay Line on Bataan, when waves of Japanese troops came forward to jump deliberately on the land mines that guarded our position, each soldier yelling *"Banzai!"* as he went to his death feet first.

The Japanese airman does not bail out—not on enemy ground. The parachute he wears is for emergencies over Japanese-held territory. You meet with occasional exceptions, so rare as to point up the steadfast rule. Now and then the lone pilot of a stricken Zero plane, far from the eyes of his leaders and fellows and caught by a sudden sense of the reality of the death that confronts him, will make the jump. I saw a few cases of Jap flyers taken prisoner. They were not good prisoners, from the point of view of our intelligence. Having saved their mortal skins, they conceded nothing more.

In New Guinea an Australian officer who had lived for years in Japan told me of giving the third degree to a Jap airman taken prisoner.

"I worked on him for two days, trying every trick and every approach," he said. "I had certain advantages: I knew the dialects and colloquialisms of every part of Japan. Now and then my knowledge would startle him, catch him in a lie or trap him into some slight admission. But he really gave nothing away. He was a spry devil, full of hell.

"I remember once I asked him if our anti-aircraft

fire didn't fill him with fear. I was trying to make him angry. He became very scornful.

" 'Anti-aircraft scares no one,' he said. 'It never hits anything. There's not one chance in a million.'

" 'But it hit you,' I pointed out.

"That brought him up for a minute, and he scratched his head. Then he just grinned.

" 'I never thought of that,' he said."

It fell to the lot of the Allied troops in the north of Australia and in Papua to be the first to see the Japs "falling" in regular consignments; to see the Zero smashed on the ground as well as the Zero in evil flight; to view the little-known enemy first-hand and dead. In the air, he was real but shapeless—speed, fire, the whine of a motor. On the ground he lay inert in his common, reducible parts, a small broken brown body in the wreckage of a small broken yellow-green piece of machinery.

In the Philippines, in Malaya, and in Java, there were too few planes—or no planes at all—to bring him down. Here it was otherwise. Our flyers had the weapons and skill to neutralize and overcome him, and he fell within easy reach of our troops on the ground. The soldiers of Darwin and Port Moresby sought out the wreckage of Zeros and bombers and came back to camp with souvenirs: pieces of wing or tail, rate-of-climb meters, bullets, gloves, shoes.

They lugged the frame of a nearly intact Zero in from the bush to the headquarters of the Royal Australian Air Force at Darwin and set it up beneath the porch of a little house there. It was the first Zero I saw on the ground: thin-skinned fuselage of yellow-green with two dark green bands, red ball on the wing, cannon in the nose, shattered glass about the cockpit. The Zeros I saw later were stronger in armament and armoring than this dead wasp, but it looked dangerous nonetheless.

A day or two later we sifted through the contents of a Mitsubishi bomber that fell hard by and found among other things a large camera in a cheap wooden case painted gray. Some English lettering had escaped obliteration: "Rokuoh-sha Color Filter." The numerals on the camera were Arabic. The Japs, I learned, almost always carried cameras of one sort or another, frequently of German, English, or American make. Their regular reconnaissance fliers are known in the Pacific, in deference to Premier Tojo, as Photo Joe.

There was one point specially noted by the air command at Darwin in the early spring. Many Japs among the bomber crews that were shot down wore bandages. This might mean something and it might not. The command, in the third year of global war against resourceful enemies, was leery of drawing spacious and rose-colored conclusions. But our fliers felt good about it, and the record, based on a cautious minimum of Japs known to be shot down or shot up, seemed to bear them out. The chain of conquest was stretched tight. Wounded Japs were sent back into action. The Pacific Ocean was a handful for even the swiftest and best-prepared of invaders.

At rare times, the enemy reversed his field and went in for strange, uncharacteristic doings, even the courtesies of war. In Port Moresby one day, in a field not far from where we watched the raid, he dropped a double sack of mail along with a number of the usual bombs, heavy stuff and daisy-cutters. The mail was from Australians held prisoner by the Japanese in Rabaul. Attached to the sacks was a suave note addressed to Australian headquarters.

"The letters are left unsealed," said the note, in part, "for the convenience of the Australian censor."

At the foot of the plain piece of white note paper was the typewritten signature: "the Japanese Headquarters."

It was a gesture which did not much interest Australian veterans of the fighting in New Guinea and the islands around it. If it contrasted with the brutalities they knew of, it did nothing to wipe those brutalities off the record.

"There was a cobber of mine captured in Rabaul," said an Australian captain. "I heard what happened to him from a native who had no cause to lie. A Jap officer asked him what outfit he belonged to. He told the truth, but the Jap didn't choose to believe him, for some reason or for no reason. Each time my pal answered, the Jap slapped his face and asked him again. Then they shot him, and then they threw him into a shallow grave and buried him there without waiting to see if he was dead. To hell with these letters from Rabaul."

XI

The Planes We Fight With

THE planes we fight with have personalities for the men who fly them. Americans, from training usage, call them by numbers: P-40, P-39, P-47, B-25, B-26, B-17, B-24, PBY. The British and Australians feel that this is a chilly attitude. They grace the flying weapons we send them with epithets of affection and esteem—Kitty-hawks ("Kitties"), Cobras, Marauders, Thunderbolts, Tomahawks, Liberators, and Cats (for Catalinas).

I never heard a love for a tool of war ring more truly than in the tone with which three Australian RAAF's (flyers of the Royal Australian Air Force) spoke one evening in Papua of the Cats and Kitties which came to their rescue against the Japanese. A Catalina Flying Boat had been destroyed in Port Moresby's harbor the day before.

"It almost made me bawl to see that Cat burning," said a wing commander.

"You did bawl," said his companion briefly.

The first Australian air fighting against the Japanese, when Tojo came down to Timor and New

Guinea, was waged in the Wirraway. The Wirraway was forced into service as Australia's only homemade pursuit plane, and it was a poor vehicle in which to discover the hidden might of the Zero. When our P-40's, the Kittyhawks, began to arrive, the Wirraway was, of course, relegated again to use as the trainer for which it was intended. It had no right in the battle zone to begin with, except the right to fight desperately and alone for the time Australia needed, when there was no other plane to do the job.

The first American pursuits to arrive in the Southwest Pacific were disappointments to American fliers there, because the Americans had expected to fly rings around the Japs, and found they couldn't. By the Australians, who had seen their comrades go to death in the Wirraway, the "Kitty" was received lovingly and gratefully. Here, at least, for a man who could fly skillfully and squeeze those big machine guns at the proper instant, was a plane that had a chance. It means everything for a flyer in a pursuit plane to have a chance in a dogfight. It changes his world.

One night four of us had drinks and talk and a dinner of bully beef with the then commander of the Allied forces in Papua, Major General Basil M. Morris. While we sat on the little veranda of the general's shack, a native boy named Jellicoe played the harmonica. Jellicoe was under missionary influence. This helped his education but hurt his music. He played with a missionary touch—long underwear, as the hepcats say. In vain the general urged him, "Cut loose with the native stuff, Jellicoe. Just relax and cut loose."

"I see, I see, now this time will be right," the fettered minstrel would say, but his music was still mired deep in the missionary cornpatch, and far from wild and true.

A big, square man suddenly pushed through the screen door and onto the veranda. The general peered at him in the dim twilight and waved Jellicoe away. The newcomer saluted.

"I've come to keep that appointment for dinner, General," he said.

He was Squadron Leader John Jackson. He had been invited to dinner two weeks before. On the morning of the dinner date he had taken off in his P-40 alone for a reconnaissance flight over the Jap bases of Lae and Salamaua, on the other side of the island. Returning, he was chased up a gully by three Zeros, and he played tag with them as long as he could, escaping out to sea again, before he ran out of fuel and crashed.

The Japs machine-gunned him in the water for a spell. Then they flew off to refuel, and Jackson made his way to shore in and around a couple of coastwise alligators. How he survived in the jungle, and how he eventually reached Moresby two weeks to the day from his first dinner date with the general, are part of a military secret that I cannot disclose even now.

Coming to dinner two weeks late, Jackson told us his story and talked in the growing darkness of his plane and her guns. He talked with almost religious zeal. Planes were all in all to him, as they were to every active fighter and ground mechanic in the region. I remember his technical argument in favor of the P-40 over the newly arrived P-39, which carried a cannon in her nose.

"Give me the Kittyhawk with those big machine guns," he said, "and you can have the cannon. I like machine guns."

There were other arguments, and talk of planes and Japs and music and "daisy-cutter" bombs, which spread hell sideways, and football and food; also, I recall, of the gambuzia, a vest-pocket fish imported to New Guinea to eat mosquito larvae, to which he is partial of a morning. The gambuzia, it develops, is surefire if he happens to get the larvae before a crayfish gets him.

Presently Jackson, tall and knobby in his shorts, plain and honest and cheerfully courteous, got up and said good-by. He was killed two days later.

"Plane was shot down," said his chief, a Wing Commander, looking blankly into his drink at the RAAF bar the evening of the day of Jackson's death. It happened often at the RAAF bar at Port Moresby that they talked over the day's score. It was usually the first place you heard the details of the cloud-veiled fighting you strained to see overhead in the daytime.

"I shouldn't have let him go up," said the Wing Commander. "Jackson had had a bad time, and besides, he was too old to fly pursuits. Quick reflexes, you know —a man must be young. Jackson was thirty-six."

Hearing his age, I remembered that Squadron Leader Jackson's hair was thin and his face slightly lined about the eyes. But he didn't seem too old to fly. Probably that was because he talked so eagerly and passionately of flying. I don't believe he wanted to stay on the ground.

Planes, individual, personal planes and their performances, were meat and drink to all that force of flyers, American and Australian, in which Jackson fought. A time is coming in the war when we will know all we need to know about planes and one type may be mass-produced for each function of aerial combat. America's first year of war was spent in learning, and the vitally significant gist of what we learned was what the different planes we made could do. That was also the vitally significant gist of what was said and heard among airmen in the Southwest Pacific in those months, when all active Army warfare was in the air and our bombers and fighters kept America's head above the Pacific waters.

Before the war, salesmen went around the world trying to sell military planes and plane equipment of one kind and another. The stuff bore company brands, like cigarettes. War came to us, and the more flagrant stigmata of salesmanship, of company brand, disappeared. If there is no discharge in war, there is no room for business rivalry. All our planes belong to us and our allies, and the only acid to test with is battle.

The B-26 is not a Martin plane, it's a plane that did this; the P-39 is not a Bell plane, it's a plane that did that. Airmen care no more for a plane's commercial background than a baseball fan cares for the lodge affiliations of a favorite ball player. The fan, however, devours the statistics of what happens in action to Medwick, to Williams, to DiMaggio. Personal statistics are half of big league baseball. If I ignored the same personal, statistical aspect of air fighting, I would ignore the very juices of our first months at war.

Knowing little about fighting planes—knowing nothing, to be starkly accurate—I came to a place where American pursuits were in daily action against the Japanese Zero. I watched them, and collected some box-scores. Then I listened to a pilot who was learning in action, flying the P-40 single-seat, low-wing monoplane that was our standard fighter in the beginning.

"The Japs' plane is better than this," he said.

This was disillusionment for me, but nothing like the disillusionment it was to the pilot in the plane.

"We were trained in the theory that we would out-maneuver and outclimb these guys," he said. "As soon as we went into action, we had to unlearn that and learn all over again. We were in something like the same spot as the Germans who came over England in the Messerschmitt and suddenly learned that the Spitfire could beat them to the draw. With our plane," the pilot said, scratching his head, "you can make one pass at the Zero. If you miss, get the hell out of there."

I am quoting "a pilot," but this fellow's remarks were repeated by dozens; all I talked to. The early P-40 got good results in many cases, in Darwin, Port Moresby, and elsewhere. Colonel Chennault's Flying Tigers made history over Burma and China with the same plane. In the Southwest Pacific our ace of pursuit fliers was Lieutenant Colonel Buzz Wagner, and his cold-blooded flying brought death to Zero after Zero.

But those were great fliers, men of genius in their work. Assuming equality in the human element, our pursuit planes were not a match for the Zero. We have better planes now, but we learned the hard way: which was the hallmark of the early fighting of unready America.

The B-17, called the Flying Fortress, was our heavy

bomber in that region. It was a stout plane and a good one in the early days. I heard of only three shot down in the air over Java and the Philippines, and I have seen the 17 land fairly at the home base with more than two hundred bullet holes in its wings and body. But the plane was not a true fortress at first, because of defensive weakness severe enough to impede its work. The first 17's had no tail armament, and Zeros swarming from behind could shoot up its equipment and personnel.

Once again, we learned. Crewmen told me with lusty relish of the first Zeros to encounter a B-17 with guns in the rear.

"They came down on our tail, up to the same old trick," said a kid with one tooth missing in the front of his jaw. "We let 'em have it, and the bastards just disintegrated."

Two of our medium bombers, the B-25 and B-26, were greeted enthusiastically from their first appearance. It was the B-25 which bombed Tokyo. Australians, who saw much of the B-26 or Marauder, called it a dream ship, and it was in many respects an exhilarating example to the depressed and punch-drunk Allies of Pacific waters of what a keen plane and a keen crew could do to an enemy so surprisingly skillful himself.

The B-26 was a "hot" plane, the fastest bomber in

the world. It needed handling. But it was beginning to get the pilots who could handle it, and I sat in the cockpit with one of them who whooped, above the roar of the motors, "She's wonderful!" He had just returned from one of those raids where the whole load hits the target. Wonderful was what he said, and wonderful was what he meant.

Thus, we fought, and learned as we fought, and gradually, over wild islands and mountains and jungle ports and sweeps of volcanic sea, our muscles began to grow firm and our eyes sharp and our knowledge to broaden. It was air war; according to our preconceived notions, it was skirmish and raid and patrol, not the big canvas of Napoleon, Lee, and Ludendorff. But the new war must have taught us by now, if we are teachable, that the air is the path to victory. Control of the air governed the great land campaigns of France, the Balkans, and Russia; the fighting in Malaya, China, and North Africa; in bold-faced type, the battle of Britain and the first onslaughts on Germany.

This has been said by students of war who know how to say it. I repeat it only as a reporter who looked and listened and could not be awake on his feet and miss the inference.

The Japanese did some learning, too, in the mighty Pacific arena; they sent out armadas of surface ships to be sunk by air. But the Japs learned at their leisure.

We had to gulp down our lesson in big, painful mouth-fuls, and gulp them we did, with the help of the friends the Australians prefer to call by Christian name, with love and respect: the Kitties, the Marauders, the Co-bras, the Fortresses, the Cats.*

* Note 3, page 292.

XII

Dakota in the Red Dust

IN the scrub jungle near Darwin we were fed and
sheltered by an American Army outfit whose soldiers
deserve the name of veterans in this war if any American troops do. Among our ground forces, only the ill-
fated garrison of the Philippines and a few scattered
units along the bloody line of Guam, Wake Island, and
Pearl Harbor came under fire sooner.

It was the luck of the draw, and these fellows took
no great satisfaction from it. Darwin was not a place for
taking satisfaction: tropic rains and mosquitoes, then
dry heat and dust; loneliness and isolation, punctuated
by Jap bombs and machine-gun fire and the sound of
our anti-aircraft and the sight of our pursuit planes
sweeping down to roost in the evening. There is a
well-known and slightly corny anecdote in circulation
about the Yank from Darwin on leave in some Australian city in the south who explained the position as
follows:

"Listen, buddy, here's how it is in Darwin. After a
while you find yourself talking to yourself. Then you

find yourself talking to the lizards. Then you find the
lizards talking to you. And pretty soon you find yourself listening."

This—"listen, buddy"—is not the way soldiers talk,
any more than you do yourself. It is part of a mythical
wartime jargon. But there is something in the lizard
story, at that. The stark emptiness of their spare hours
drove the Yanks in Darwin to strange pursuits, like
the sergeant and private from our camp who could
think of nothing to do but go off in the bush and shoot
at alligators with their .45 revolvers. They were lost
for three days.

There was not a woman within fifty miles, save for
the occasional Aboriginal lubra who stole back among
the camps to beg tobacco. Darwin's town was a vacant
shell. The sun burned without interruption by day—
when the dry season came at the start of April—and
along the Burma Road winding south through the bush
the red dust seeped into your hair, your ears, and every
exposed crevice of your body. Your correspondent,
stirred by this phenomenon, answered the request of
our hosts for a regimental song by composing a madri-
gal to the tune of *Red Sails in the Sunset,* which began:

> Red dust in your navel,
> Red dust in your shirt;
> See beautiful Darwin
> For beautiful dirt.

What struck you was the steady cheerfulness and quiet competence with which these young soldiers from the Middle West carved themselves a home in the jungle and settled down to work and wait, side by side with their comrades from America and the rough and ready Diggers, for the invasion that was expected for some months to follow the bombs and the Zeros into Darwin.

Socially, our first boys to reach Darwin were among friends. Architecturally, they were on their own. They built their camp to suit their special purposes. They improved the tracks and overgrown rutted "roads" in their part of the bush, or built new tracks. They set up their own tents, huts, and shacks. They spread a bed of concrete in a jungle clearing and built shower-baths in the open air and troughs for washing and shaving. They made their own latrines.

"The sanitation around here is terrific," said Colonel Leslie Jensen modestly.

Jensen was the commander of "our" outfit. He was a tall, thin, baldish, gentle-spoken man who had once been governor of South Dakota—Republican, I will add, at the risk of seeming redundant. For Allen Raymond and me, the first American correspondents to reach Darwin and therefore the first to settle down upon the colonel and claim his hospitality, he broke open a bottle of youthful Muscatel, the last of its kind or any other kind in the region, and did some patient figuring.

"There is a spot just back of my shack here," said the colonel. "I will have 'em put up a tent for you fellows."

"Let us do it," said Raymond, always the dreamer.

The colonel saw this suggestion for the bright but unattainable ideal that it was, and shook his head.

"No, our boys will take care of it," he said. "Then, by the time the other two men you speak of get here, we will have a shack fixed for them over there some place. Imposition? Boy, if you don't know what news and new faces and a little exchange of conversation can mean up here, you don't know Darwin."

Most of the Dakotans and their American neighbors fore and aft of the camp had had no mail since they left home, nor were there any facilities at the time for sending mail or cables out of Darwin. When we finally broke camp there, we went away loaded with messages to be posted or cabled at the nearest civilized spot. Things got better later, and the Darwin garrison was assigned a B-17 for its own uses, to fetch and carry mail.

The day in Darwin the Dakotans remembered best, of course, was February 19, the day the town and port were brutally blasted from their torpor. Nearly every man had some small souvenir of the shambles—if only a piece of shrapnel picked up or dug from the ground. Then the Jap became a daily guest, and these collections took on range and color: everything from pencils (Japanese) to compasses (Japanese).

Pursuing our own investigations, we always came home to the "Hotel Dakota" at dusk and found companionship and information in the pitch-black but cheerful night life of the camp. More often than not we messed with Colonel Jensen and his comrades. It was the simplest sort of fare, but abundant. The young chefs from the Black Hills attained the apex of their art in the early morning, with hot cakes. A young cameraman named Frank Prist, who joined up with us temporarily, went to bed one night convinced beyond rebuttal that his body was racked with dengue fever, but the perfume of hot cakes had him out of the hay and into the mess shack the next morning in one minute and two-fifths seconds. His work with the knife and fork convinced his physician that Prist was as dengue-less a photographer as could be found in those hills.

We got ice cream one evening, much to the astonishment of the commanding officer. It developed that Lieutenant "Doc" Loy, a cop in private life and a genius with his ten fingers, had constructed an ice cream freezer out of spare truck parts and a piece of a Japanese bomber plane.

Loy became a father after he left home. He was lucky enough to get a letter enclosing a snapshot of his new baby, and from the photograph, Lance Corporal John McCormack drew a life-size head of the child. McCormack also sketched Colonel Jensen and most of his aides. He was a brash but enterprising little fellow, McCormack, and the best artist in Australia; I had his personal word for that.

"There's no one in this country can touch me," said Mac as he sat in front of my tent, sketching a poker game in a nearby slit trench. "Of course, the field is not highly developed."

McCormack was the first example I saw of personal ambassadorship between Australian soldiers and Americans. He got permission from his commander in the Australian Engineers to attach himself to the Dakota troops in their camp, and he attached himself with firmness. He was ingratiating and knowing and coolly observant for a youth of twenty-one, and he soon knew more about the private lives and histories of the men than any officer in the outfit.

"They probably talk to me because they realize I know life," said Mac. "Also, I speak their language."

That was true enough. McCormack had mastered American ways of speech. He was the only Australian soldier the boys knew thereabouts who pronounced the first letter of the alphabet "ay" instead of "eye." And he was handy at repairing gadgets and doing camouflage work.

The Japs bombed us Easter Sunday—"rolled eggs on the lawn," as the troops lost no time pointing out. The raid was short, and soon the phonograph began to play again near the kitchen shack, the same few records over and over, songs that sounded nostalgic in the hot jungle as rendered by nasal but well-meaning troubadors: *Come Back to the Valley, Rose Marie, Hear That Old Freight Train, Rolling Down the Mountain, I Never Saw the Fellow Who Could Ride Aristocrat.*

The camp was low on cigarettes that week—just enough Piedmonts to go around. At night a few dozen of the men and officers would cluster around the radio truck set up across the road from the showers, and there, smoking in the moonlight, standing in the grass or sitting against the roots of scrubby eucalyptus trees, they listened to the only news that reached them from the outside world: short wave broadcasts from San Francisco. This program didn't always come through; often it was submerged by static or the curt pronouncements of the Tokyo radio.

A few nights after Easter came the crowning event of our stay, the rarest and highest treat within reach of the men of Dakota camped in the Darwin jungle. The regimental swing band gave a concert. The night, following a day without bombs, was moonlit, and the Southern Cross blazed above. The musicians brought their guns as well as their instruments. They took their seats in a double row in the center of a clearing, and around them a circle of hundreds of men took form, sitting, standing, perched in trees, faces intent and white in the moonlight, banked in rows as far as the shadow of the bush that fenced the clearing.

There were troops from other camps. There were Diggers, hugging their knees as they sat in the front rows and watched the players with absorption. Much of the songs and jive they heard was new to them. So were the antics of the band. Good swing bands are rare in Australia, and this was a good one.

It had three saxophones, three trumpets, two trombones, drums, and bass horn. It was Dakota's own. Some of the musicians had gone through college together, and their college instructor, now the regiment's bandleader, stood leaning against a tree in the background, listening approvingly to the boys as they warmed up and then went swinging to town.

"This stuff," said an officer beside me, "is the biggest thing in the lives of the boys here. Only trouble is, it makes them think of their girls at home, and they look a little mopey next day."

The band got the bugs out of the horns. It struck the groove and grew warm and sure with *Boogly*

Woogly Piggy, Green Eyes, Song of India, Whispering, From Taps to Reveille, and the boys' theme song, *White Heat.* The rapt audience yelled out request numbers, and broke into cheers when the first trumpet, slim and black-haired, rose to play his solo licks. I recommend this fellow to the attention of Goodman and Dorsey. He will be worth investigating when the war is over. The leader and vocalist was equally good when he put down his saxophone and sang and jittered to boisterous applause in front of the band.

In the midst of the concert the band saluted its Digger guests with a slow and halting performance of *Bless 'Em All.* The Australians acknowledged the anthem with pleasure. But then, they took pleasure in everything played. It was a big night in the jungle.

I heard that the band had had local rivalry earlier in the year from the Aboriginals in a patch of bush several miles away—the only other swing musicians on the Darwin peninsula. The Abos had drummed and swung in a special festival, in honor of a boy tribesman about to become a man. Some of the Dakotans went over to watch.

"They were pretty good," said the band leader. "Jimmy, our drummer, picked up a few points."

In the afternoons of those days in the South Dakota camp, before the sun could get too low, we flagged Sergeant Bill Bailey, the nimble Texas driver, and rolled off down the Burma Road to the tent of the Australian censor who checked and filed our stories—a gentleman who buried his camp so skillfully in the bush that we almost had to call on an Abo tracker to find him the first time. He was a lieutenant, or leftenant, and visibly depressed by the amounts of copy we handed him.

"What quantity, what quantity!" he would mutter, leafing the stuff.

"But does it go through?"

"It goes through me nicely," he said, mopping his brow. "I can't answer for the other three censors between here and the States."

That was the beauty of filing from Darwin. Only four men censored your writings en route. From New Guinea it was five, or just enough for a basketball team, though none of the boys, as I happen to know, played basketball.

The tenor of life in Darwin was such that our Dakota hosts, men and officers both, often asked to read our stories before we sent them; figuring, no doubt, that it was just as good as shooting at alligators with .45's, and less risky. They even paid us the compliment of reprinting some of those stories in a newssheet they circulated about the camp.

"It is good, clean stuff," said Lieutenant Doc Loy

handsomely, "and nothing in it I wouldn't let a sergeant read."

We left the brave and dusty campers one morning and rattled off southward with Sergeant Bailey at the wheel to look for a plane that would fly us elsewhere. From Colonel Jensen down the line, the Dakotans yelled us a lusty sendoff. Shirtless and barelegged, burned to mahogany shades by the jungle sun, they stood there guarding the path to a continent eight thousand miles from home. When we last saw them, a couple of privates by the roadside were practicing passes with the only American football that existed on Darwin peninsula, as of April, 1942.

XIII

As the Dutchman Flies

WOMEN henna their hair for reasons best known to themselves. By the time we reached the airfield we were bound for, fringed by dry bush and the north Australian desert, the four of us were in a state of redheadedness bordering on involuntary Titian or reluctant pigeon's-blood. Only one of the troupe, Knickerbocker, had been born that way, and he at a time when he was too young to know better.

Raking the carmine topsoil out of our manes, along with some north Australian flora, a couple of fauna, and the best part of a jeep that passed us on the windblown road, we contemplated with pity the lot of redheaded people past and present, such as Mickey Rooney, Queen Elizabeth (the Tudor) of England, Barbarossa, Red Grange, Eric the Red, Ann Sheridan, William the Conqueror's son Rufus, Charlie Ruffing, and Man o' War.

A showerbath is not much good, because the minute you step outside you look like Mickey Rooney again. And Rooney is paid lavish sums for looking that way, which lightens his burden somewhat. With desert red-headedness, you are lucky if you break even.

We ran into a beer stampede at the airfield. The Australian troops stationed at that dusty junction had waited a long time since their last beer ration, and now the queue stretched a hundred yards down the steps and along the road from the supply window. Naked and brown from nose to waist and knee to shoe, supple and finely-muscled under their floppy broad-brimmed hats, the Diggers looked ahead with tense eyes as they came in sight of the counter. When the precious bottles were in their hands, they bore them off exultantly, and with great speed, to their quarters.

There were three bottles left over when the last Aussie departed. Standing forlorn and redhaired (non vult) on the edge of the scene, we were filled with half-believing joy by the sudden offer of the commissary clerk.

"Take these, Yanks," he said, shoving the bottles over the counter. "You're breaking my bloody heart."

We picked up the bottles. They were nice and warm.

"Thank you very much."

"Never mind bloody thank you," said the clerk handsomely. "You're richly bloody welcome. Better take salt tablets with the stuff."

We lugged the steaming lager back to the tent where the four of us had been berthed for the night, to wait for our plane. We figured that one of the bottles couldn't wait, parboiled or not. The other two we invested with the keeper of the kitchen icebox, with the touching faith of depositors leaving bonds with their banker for safekeeping. In the morning we would have cold beer.

In the morning, however, when we called at the bank, the vault was devoid of Pilsener. The chef threw open the wooden door and peered inside.

"No beer," he announced.

"No beer?"

"No —— beer," said the master of the kitchen, drawing upon that crisp but slightly unprintable participle which the Digger substitutes for "bloody" when he speaks in true earnest.

"But we deposited the stuff with you last night. Two full bottles. You remember that, don't you?"

The chef kicked the door of the icebox shut and tapped a rich philosophical vein.

"This is war," he said. "With bloody thirsty Yanks to the left of you and bloody thirsty Aussies to the right of you, you can't expect to put beer away in a crib like this and find it again in the morning. Besides," said the chef austerely, "what do you want to chill bloody beer for? What's wrong with warm beer?"

We stumbled away, convicted on fourteen counts of Sybaritism. And the chef and his assistant turned nonchalantly back to an argument they had been having when we interrupted them. It sounded very interesting.

"Oh, definitely —— yes," said the chef.

"Definitely —— not," said his assistant.

"I say definitely —— yes," said the chef.

They were still hard at it by lunchtime.

This was an airdrome hewn swiftly out of the bush and desert when war came to Australia. It was a masterpiece of engineering work—one of several we saw in the north country, where American Engineer outfits startled their fellow Yanks as well as the frankly admiring Aussies by their efficiency. Digging, trucking, mixing, rolling the materials themselves, cutting swaths in the live jungle, they created smooth runways big enough to accommodate the biggest bomber, camouflaged them, built dispersal outlets and auxiliary fields, and in some cases put their signatures to the finished and polished miracle six weeks from the day they cut the first tree.

"Simply marvelous," said the Australian gunnery commander at the field where we waited. He was tall, thin, leather-brown, a veteran of the Libyan campaign. Like many Aussies who had come home from the Middle East when the Japs began to bark, he was just beginning to concede that the Australians and Yanks down here might between them muster something approaching the skills and science of the desert fighters in Africa.

He took us on a tour of his gun emplacements. We began to realize that Australia, for all the thinness of her resources at that early time and the honest pleas of her government for more help, was in a fair way to becoming a tough nut to crack.

"Soon," said our lanky guide, "this matter of invasion of Australia will be the Jap's worry, not ours."

Some of the guns were manned by American anti-aircraft outfits. I recognized them: kids who had sailed here on the same convoy with me. They'd been green and awkward then, fiddling with new machine guns, learning the ropes, wondering what war held in store for them; something like freshmen on the train to college in September. Now, just a few weeks later, they were veterans of a sort. They had seen fire, they were toughened and competent, they took a lively interest in artillery and flying problems and the terrain. This terrain could have been the blistered backend of the universe—it looked a little like that—and still have won the affection of these particular men from scattered regions of New England and New York and the South. It was their first battlefield.

We camped one more night there. Then we heard that the Dutchman was ready to go.

Out on a runway in the sun sat a big DC5 plane.

Beside it, in a camp-chair in the shade of a wing, sat Captain Hans Smits. He looked neat and cool in his white silk shirt and brown shorts. He was a highly impassive character. He nodded. Other Netherlanders showed us where to stow our stuff in the plane, while Smits sat and stared abstractedly down the runway. Pretty soon a ground crew rolled forth in a truck to gas us up.

Smits was neither melancholy nor meditative, we found. He was simply resting. He took his rest where he could. Freighting cargo about Australia in the plane he had snatched from the wreckage of Java, he had been in the air one hundred and twenty-five hours in the last ten days alone while most of his time on the ground was given to loading, administering, seeing the right people, and repairing and nursing his ship. That very morning he had bounced fifty miles in a jeep up the red "Burma Road" and back again in search of a new tire. He would take off now, land somewhere for fresh cargo, take off again, land somewhere else, load again. He would fly till his brain and eyes and the bones in his body mutinied.

What drove him? Japan has no more faithful and implacable enemy in the world than the Dutch in Pacific waters. With them, the memory of the rape of Java is reinforced by the thought of ruin and carnage in the homeland. Families and property—both precious to the

Dutch—were lost. Those who escaped to work and fight elsewhere will spare no effort to avenge the one and regain the other.

Smits and other pilots brought their DC5's out of Java. They are Douglas planes built especially for the Indies service. To the end of defeating the enemy, they gave their special talent: there are no commercial flyers in the world more skillful than those of the Netherlands East Indies. They leased the planes to the American Army and flew them themselves. It was as good to win the war in one place as another; if work could do it, it would be done.

The heat and dust of the desert, we noticed, failed miserably to ruffle the neatness of Smits and his crew. We were glad we had got our shirts and pants cleaned the day before at Doyle's Never Never Aboriginal Laundry, where Mr. Doyle, bushwhacker, administered the work of three lubras, Mary, Rose, and Mary II, at the jungle's edge.

A sergeant, in a jeep, pulled up beside Smits' chair and asked the Dutchman politely to move his ship to another runway to make room for P-40's about to take off at the end of this one. Smits glanced over his shoulder at the fighter planes, then measured the runway with his eye.

"That will lose me time," he said. "They have room."

They had, at that.

Leaving the ground the moment the gas was in the tanks, we flew through the afternoon and into the night. Knickerbocker and I played gin rummy in the bare interior of the plane. The ship vibrated ominously. This was traceable not to the motors but to Allen Raymond, snoring in a cot just forward. Ralph Jordan, sleeping in the cot beside him for want of better accommodation, shook like Santa Claus's belly from the force of Raymond's mighty pipe-organ tones. The crew observed this phenomenon with admiration and slept when it found time. Smits flew on, sleepless, over wasteland and jungle.

Toward midnight we came down on civilized ground, on the airfield of a quiet Queensland town, to refuel and check the plane and await further flying orders. Smits got out and talked to the ground hands. We found we had time to go into town and eat, and we asked him if we could bring him back some sandwiches and tea. Smits smiled for the first time since we had met him.

"All right," he said.

Then he stretched out in the plane and went to sleep. His co-pilot stretched on a blanket on the ground beside the ship and went to sleep. Rip Van Winkle never slumbered sounder.

This was Friday night, Australia's night out—which

doesn't mean that an inland town as small as this one was burning much oil after midnight. We found one restaurant open, ate steak and eggs and milk shakes, and were laying out cards on the table for a game when the cab driver mentioned a Friday night dance in progress at the town hall a few blocks away. There were American soldiers there, he said. It was the first we knew that the Yanks had reached this town. They were there in quantity, as it turned out. However, when we found them, they were not exactly tearing the town apart.

The front doors of the town hall were half open. Through them to the street came light and the sound of music. A truckload of colored troops rattled by in the night, the passengers leaning overboard to catch a glimpse of the dance. We noticed two M.P.'s on patrol in front of the hall. Then we walked in and beheld a singular sight. The widely heralded dash and élan of Yank soldiers in Australia were not operating as advertised.

At the far end of the dance floor a woman was thumping the piano and a gaunt civilian sawed the fiddle. The lights were bright and the tunes were gay, square-dance tunes, but the dancers were almost exclusively girls, paired off together in the steps of the communal turkey-trot. There were working girls and farm girls and high school girls, all in their best party dresses, their low-hemmed Friday night finery. They were nice to see, too. That is a condition you can bank on almost anywhere in Australia. But the few male partners to be seen among them were local civilians, to a man.

The American Army hugged the wall, enfiladed in chairs all around the floor and in the reception room outside. Here and there a girl sat between two soldiers, but she might as well have been stationed between the two stone lions in front of the New York Public Library.

It was a harrowing sight, this mass attack of shyness. It may have been induced by the square dances, or by the fact that the boys were new in town. I hasten to add that it was unique in my investigations of Australia and that the situation may have improved as the night wore on. Just before we left, a corporal faced the issues squarely and led a handsome maiden out on the floor. This move toward gaining the initiative probably led to a general advance, but we couldn't wait to see it.

When we reached the plane in the darkness, Smits and the co-pilot were still asleep. The plane had been gassed, flight directions were ready, and the field hand called to Smits. He awoke instantly. So did the co-pilot. Smits smoothed back his hair with his hand and walked toward the controls. When we gave him tea and sandwiches he nodded briefly and stowed them near by.

He was wasting no time. In another minute the Dutchman had her in the air again.

It was dawn when we came over Brisbane, spreading white and red at the foot of green coastal hills and along the serpentine Brisbane River, winding out to sea. Smits brought her down carefully. I know of a U.S. Transport Command plane that was fired at from the ground, coming in to Brisbane. And the city was not overly itchy with her trigger finger. Such things have happened in the East Indies, before they fell, and in India, China, Scotland, and even England. It is a hazard that the pilots of the world face with proper caution but with resignation. In war, groundlings do not wait for bombs to tell them who is who.

We landed, and Hans Smits dropped quickly to the ground behind us, still neat and imperturbable.

"What do you do now?" I asked him.

The Dutchman rested one hand against the door of the plane for a moment.

"I see about loading again," he said.

Then he walked briskly away across the field.

XIV

City Life

LENNON'S HOTEL had run away with its manager, Mrs. Shaughnessy, and gone Hollywood. Each time the elevator reached the lobby floor it debouched more generals, colonels, air heroes, army doctors, nurses, flying Dutchmen, society belles, reporters, cameramen, airline hostesses, and international nomads than a scenario writer could shake a stick at.

Being a lady of firm character, Mrs. Shaughnessy fought back, and was never completely trampled by the herd of War-time Cosmopolitan Characters, Inbound, or the herd of War-time Cosmpolitan Characters, Outbound. From her desk she called hopefully to everyone who crossed the lobby:

"When are you leaving?"

If you called back "Right away," Mrs. Shaughnessy rubbed her hands and shot you a grateful smile. If you said "Not for a while yet," she sank back in her chair and muttered "Lord save us."

The hotel's war-time atmosphere—which was one of relaxation with a sharp bang—she had begun to take in stride. But a traffic problem imposed itself on the hoorah. For every colonel or pilot or man with a mission who checked out, Mrs. Shaughnessy saw two colonels, three pilots, or four men with missions waiting in line at the desk. And when she did sell a "vacant" room or suite, the new tenant was apt to find somebody there before him who invoked squatter's rights at the top of his lungs—or primogeniture or hereditary law.

"Lieutenant Claffey gave me the room when he left last night."

"He gave it to you?" said the startled landlady, attempting to arbitrate.

"Yes, ma'am. He wants you to hold his laundry, and I'll pay for the broken chair. Look now, if you could send up a plate of sandwiches and a bottle of beer..."

Running her fingers desperately through her cloudy dark hair, Mrs. Shaughnessy would concede defeat and lead her new client away with a hint of a possible vacancy Friday. Meanwhile, there was a very comfortable lodging-house just a few blocks up Queen Street...."

Lennon's, built in the heart of the friendly seaport of Brisbane, new and shiny, with automatic elevators and chromium trimmings and red leather in the lounge bar, was not meant to compete with Shepheard's in Cairo or the Grand Hotel of Vicki Baum. It was meant to be the "best" hotel of a pleasant Australian city of 300,000-odd population, and as such the rendezvous of sober local society and the nicer types of visitor and wayfarer. Till 1942 it served those ends nobly, rejoicing the heart of the lady whom I call Mrs. Shaughnessy to identify the land of her ancestors.

Then came the Pacific war. It caught up Lennon's and spun the place like a top. Brisbane sits astride the lane from Australia's war zone in the north to headquarters in the south. Leaders and strategists pass through, coming and going, with their retinues. Flyers come down from the north on leave. Army doctors and supply officers and specialists and emissaries and men on secret assignments touch at Brisbane, as well as the general war traffic of sea, rail, and air, both civilian and military—Australian, American, Dutch. And to touch at Brisbane is to touch at Lennon's and clamor for the bemused hospitality of Mrs. Shaughnessy.

No inn in the Southwest Pacific can contest Lennon's position as the foremost social arena and carrousel of the war. Mrs. Shaughnessy would welcome rivals. It is no satisfaction to this honest lady to reflect that even the Japanese have heard of Lennon's. The Tokyo radio spokesman singled it out some months ago and paid tribute to the fame of Mrs. Shaughnessy's signboard.

"We will send planes to Brisbane," he said with unction, "and administer to Lennon's Hotel a special bombing. The bar is full of characters who will shortly be blown to bits."

This, it turned out, was an empty boast, and Japanese bombs remain the only fireworks of any description that have yet to explode in Lennon's.

In the lobby you thread your way through trunks, bedrolls, and musette bags, tacking carefully around the 'Ouse-Porter, a fellow whose nerves have been wrecked by the boom. He is snarling for "young bloody Albert" or "young bloody Jimes," pageboys three feet high, to come and carry a trunk upstairs or find a cab (Australia's equivalent of the Golden Fleece). You approach the automatic elevators and begin a game which takes the place of slot machines at Lennon's.

You push a button, and the car at the fourth floor starts down. It stops at the second, takes on a load of Dutch pilots, and goes up to the fifth. Meanwhile, the other car has descended as far as the third floor, where a general and his aides embark and go up to the fourth. Once every twenty minutes you hit the jackpot: a car reaches the lobby. By the time its contents have been disgorged, however, and the last man out has forgotten to hold the door open, the elevator is purring upward without you in response to a call from the fifth floor—doubtless to be intercepted at the third by five hungry nurses bound for the dining-room on the second.

There is scattered betting in the lobby on these elevators, the standard odds being 9 to 1 that a car will not get all the way down on two pushes of the button and 5 to 1 that it won't make it in three tries. A score in the first inning is a 20-to-1 shot. There being two cars, you can make any number of parlay bets. Mrs. Shaughnessy was cold to a suggestion that she post a house bookmaker in front of the elevator shaft to cash in on the possibilities.

"There is nothing droll in this state of affairs," she said, and turned to brush off two majors at the head of the waiting line.

The house had a curfew rule—no outsiders, especially ladies, admitted after 6 P.M. This led to an interesting scene each evening at 5:45, when the doors burst open and a stampede of non-guests swept into the lobby and scattered in all directions, to be assimilated by fifty different house parties. There was no rule against leaving the hotel when you wanted. Mrs. Shaughnessy was enthusiastically in favor of anybody leaving at any time.

The food was only so-so after Lennon's lost its Italian chef toward the start of the war. The swarm of American customers had a dynamic effect on dining-room service: the handmaidens learned to bring drinking water to the table without a special order. If Yanks had to drink water with their meals, it was all right with the management; Yanks were funny. That is, they were funny up to a point. Beyond that point, several miles beyond it, came the pyramids of cigarette butts, the shoals of glassware, and the occasional semicadaver that confronted the chambermaids of a morning.

Mrs. Shaughnessy came to accept these and other phenomena as indivisible from Yanks at play—Yanks and the likes of Yanks. I saw her shocked only once, and that was through an innocent request of my own, for a Bible. Writing a story in my room one night, I tried to remember the number of the Commandment which says "Thou shalt not kill." I was pretty sure it was the Sixth, but not dead certain. I telephoned down for the house Testament. Half an hour of painful pause ensued, till Albert, the microscopic pageboy, appeared with a copy of Scripture which he said he had gone down the street to borrow from the Presbyterian Mission a few blocks away. The flyleaf of the book supported his testimony.

Mrs. Shaughnessy was chilly as steel the following morning. Toward noon, when I went to the desk to pick up my key, she fired a leading question. Indignation blazed from her eyes.

"Don't you chaps find enough devilment," she said, "without making wagers on the Bible?"

I hastily pleaded not guilty and explained the state of the case. She considered my story. The truth appeared to satisfy her. Then I perceived that embarrassment, as much as anything else, underlay the landlady's feeling about a Bible ordered at night, à la room service. What distressed her—no matter how frivolous she thought the request to be—was the revelation that Lennon's had no Bible.

"I meant to have the Book in every room," she mourned. "A fine place good people will take this to be. Not that we've had many good people since you Yanks came," she added sternly. "This is the first request for the Bible."

Brisbane, for men and officers alike, is a fine place to camp or spend leave. Down by the harbor you can buy stone crabs or mud crabs in quantities, cheap, that make fine eating. Because she lies well in from the sea, Brisbane is not one of the great surfing centers of Australia, but there are good enough beaches not too far distant. You can even swim in the river—if you take the precaution to go to one of the little rectangular compounds of water that are palisaded off from the sharks.

Australia is fertile Salvation Army country. At the public beaches and shore resorts of a Sunday you will see crowds of solemnly attentive children gathered around a Salvation Army minstrel who is teaching them a new hymn or reviewing them on past lessons— a little coyly sometimes, in the fashion of Uncle Don, the pied pianist of American radio, but always to the nodding satisfaction of the children's parents who watch from benches near by.

Soldiers occasionally find their way to the zoo on a

hilltop called Mount Coot-tha, outside the city, where the lady proprietor and her handsome daughter exhibit cheerfully, for a nominal fee, their compact stock of kangaroos, wallabies, koala bears, bright-colored birds, and carpet snakes. More easily the troops find their way to the movie houses and bars downtown, and to the postoffice. The postoffice is a Yank soldier's forum and his first stop on leave, since it handles telegraph and cable messages as well as ordinary mail. Australia has arranged special rates and special forms for American soldiers cabling home, but it was still a pretty doleful process when I was there—the wires to and from cable centers, and the cable and radio channels across the sea, were so laden with military priority matter that a soldier never knew when his message would reach home or when an answer would come—except that he knew it would be a powerful long time.

If there is one thing Yanks abroad pine for news of, it is sports at home; especially in the spring and summer months when the major league baseball races are run. The Australian newspapers do their best to accommodate. Newsprint is strictly rationed, and even the biggest Australian papers run to no more than six or eight pages these days, so that news of baseball results in America must be telescoped. Sir Keith Murdoch, Australia's principal journalistic tycoon, told me they were giving it all the space the traffic would bear. This, in such cities as Brisbane, Melbourne, and Sydney, came to a slim column three or four days a week, in agate type, which supplied the boys with a rough idea of what was transpiring on the horsehide front as soon as they learned to decode the cheerful baseball rhetoric of the Anzacs, e.g.:

"Dickey of the St. Louis Yankees ran home with two on bases making three over the plate. The Yankees beat St. Louis."

In their state of enforced leanness, the papers could offer little but headline war news, editorials, stories of the war's effect domestically, a few random comic strips, and a page of racing news. No matter how much respect a publisher felt for the Japanese menace, he knew the hot breath of the enemy would actually have to singe the collars of his readers before they would dispense with racing news. So he supplied it, as publishers will: five or six days of advance data on Saturday's races, and then, on Sunday or Monday, a fat catalogue of results—with a separate headline and story for each race on the program, each narrative a mighty and full-blooded saga of the adventures of the twelve or fifteen graceless hayburners who stole the money of the doting public, epics worthy of Beowulf or Sohrab and Rustam or Tom Brown's first boat race or the Fall of Man and the loss of Paradise.

There is not much difference between the Australian horse bug and his American "off-sider," or counterpart; except that the Australian feels more affection for the horse as a horse and can generally tell one animal from another without reference to the number on his back. He genuflects to the bronze idol of betting, but not quite so abjectly. The Australian racing reporter, therefore, can be less cynical and more heroic in his prose than the American writer, though he seldom falls into the "sportin'" hypocrisy of some of the American horse critics who keep one hand on the keyboard and the other in the Jockey Club's pocket.

The comic strip field is thin, there being no strip with sufficient calories to replace *Terry and the Pirates* or *Blondie* or *Superman* or *L'il Abner*. The best of them are *Ben Bowyang*, a country-store comic that has authentic outback Australian flavor in its talk, and a strip of Digger life called *Bluey and Curly*. (N.B. In Australia the nickname "Bluey" is applied to people of redheaded persuasion. "Bluey" and the American "Red" are synonymous, and it seems fitting that the great Melbourne football hero, Bluey Truscott, now with the RAF, is just as pink as our own Red Grange.)

You could detect, especially in the first months of Yank mobilization in Australia, an uneasiness among Australian newspaper men over the "suppression" of certain Australian domestic news for export. In fact, they began to complain about it, and to call attention to shoals off the censor's starboard helm.

Australian papers printed news of Australian wartime labor troubles—which existed. They told of the discovery and trial of a fifth column organization called Australia First—which existed. They reported the hot squabbles in Parliament over the fact that the Australian Militia, which formed the larger part of the country's armed force, could not legally be sent to fight on foreign soil—which was true. While these stories were fully published and openly discussed in Australia, however, the local censorship forbade any mention of them in dispatches to America. The attitude of the censorship seemed to be that if Australia was not represented in the United States as the garden spot of human virtue, a patch of heaven on earth, with seraphim playing the harp on every convenient corner and cherubs matching coins in the middle distance, American sympathy for Australia would subside and American help stop flowing southwestward.

The newspapers rebuked the censor, and pointed out a gruesome possibility: that American correspondents in Australia would go home, slip off the handcuffs, and Tell All with the blackest ink at their disposal.

The censor's stand was certainly silly. It struck me,

though, as a good example of the nervous confusion that infects free and peaceful nations when they are suddenly forced to re-learn the dark arts of war. Australia, strongly and efficiently unionized, had her labor conflicts; it would have been startling if she hadn't. Her "Australia First" movement was trifling, comic, and bush-league compared with some of our own Fascist excrescences before Pearl Harbor. The Parliamentary quarrel about the Militia could be matched weekly by half a dozen unlovely spats in Congress. I saw no reason to doubt the reliability of a political reporter who told me that as soon as it became necessary for the militamen to fight abroad, they would do so.

An American correspondent returning from Australia to "lift the lid" can only say that Australia is not heaven on earth, nor is it peopled exclusively by paid-up saints in good standing. It's a good deal more homey than that.

If the Yank in Brisbane and elsewhere missed Moon Mullins in his newspaper and had to settle for Bluey and Curly, he could get all the Hollywood produce he wanted. Australian cinemas carry little else but American films—almost always in double-feature doses. They packed 'em in, Yanks, Diggers, and civilians, though the Yank was disgruntled to find that his red day, Sunday, was a blue day here, without movies. An Australian

editorial writer, stirred by the sight of American troops
wandering sadly and hopelessly through city streets
on the Sabbath, denounced the Sundays of his native
land.

"Nowhere else in the world," he thundered, "is there
anything to match the inspissated gloom of this insti-
tution."

He spoke a mouthful there.

Patrolling Brisbane on sunny weekday mornings, the
Yank soldier found that a "casket agency" was a place
where you bought lottery tickets. He found that you
go to tobacco shops to get haircuts; and that you did
not get cigarettes at all unless your own canteen happened to be stocked with smokes from America. The
first soldiers to arrive in Australia saw their first
WAAFS there, the Australian variety of *WAAC*—and a
very impressive spectacle, too. Some of these ladies
drove the busses of the shuttle service between Lennon's Hotel and U.S. Army Headquarters in Brisbane.
It was well worth the trip to see the broad-shouldered
driver brake a big command car in front of headquarters, stretch a powerful assortment of biceps, and then
take her compact from the seat beside her and begin
to powder her nose.

"This business of dames in uniform will never catch
on at home," said a major, one of the commanding

officer's aides, as he dropped off the bus. "It's not practical."

"Why not?" I asked.

"I don't know," growled the major, pulling his garrison cap down over his eyes. "I'm just whistling through the graveyard, kid."

XV

Log of the Firecracker

IT was night when we first saw the freighter, wheezing gently through her tackle alongside a dock in Brisbane while the longshoremen hoisted bombs into her forward hold. Each bomb, long and yellow, hovered a few moments against the sky before it began its mincing descent through the open hatch to the hold.

The third officer led us up the gangway, then along the port rail and down to the mouth of a hold amidships, where our bags were stowed. Back against the wall were big red drums mounted in double rows—high octane gasoline.

"That's the cargo, bombs and gasoline," said the Third. "You got cots? All right, just set 'em up in the open space here, where you find room, and make yourself at home."

There was a shirt and a towel draped over one of the gas drums. They belonged to a young soldier who lay on a cot in a corner, stripped to his shorts. Alongside the high octane on the wall he had spread his posters from Hawaii—pretty Eurasian girls on the beach—and a map of Australia and the islands to the north. We started unpacking and setting up the cots.

"Don't smoke in here," said the third officer, moving off. "The chief told me to tell you. Just for his peace of mind. There's fumes circulating from that gasoline."

She got her name of *Floating Firecracker* from Allen Raymond, one of the ten men—five Army gunners and five waifs of the press—who roomed with those big red drums on the voyage to Port Moresby. She was 5,200 tons and could do 11 knots in a hurry. Before the war, she and her captain hauled paper, newsprint, along the Pacific Coast. The captain had no complaints, but I think the ship missed the Coast run and her load of newsprint, for now and then, when a squall blew up off the Coral Sea, she groaned in her patient, plodding course.

Maybe this was because of the "Sleepwalker." The Sleepwalker joined us on hot nights, when we pitched the cots outdoors on the hatch above the forward hold. The Sleepwalker was a rogue bomb that pulled himself aloof from the herd and rolled below us, forward and aft, when the ship pitched. Raymond called him "Old Restless," but the name was a little forced, a little stuffy, and did not do the author credit. In Raymond's defense, you have to realize that he was beginning to read the short stories of Thomas Mann for the first time. His nimble mind was slightly benumbed.

The library found a place on top of the gasoline drums, along with our shirts, towels, socks and the gunners' haberdashery. Besides Mann, Raymond discovered *Delilah* by Marcus Goodrich. Knickerbocker read Huxley's *Ends and Means* and wrestled a fall or two with *Les Chouans* of Balzac. Someone had brought along a stray volume of assorted Russian short stories. There was no sunnier, gayer correspondent in the Southwest Pacific than Ralph Jordan, but Jordan, like the volatile morning-glory, needed the sun to exist. Hourly, as he read the Russian stories, his face grew grayer and more wretched.

He finally took to standing at the rail for long spells and staring at the sky or the distant atolls. I believe he got as far as page 129 before quitting.

I had Parkman's *Conspiracy of Pontiac* to read, and thought the great historian belittled the character of the great Indian. Earle Crotchett didn't read much. Crotch, Universal Newsreel man, stood guard over his hundreds of pounds of equipment, or wrote in his diary, or played the radio. One night over this radio, under millions of stars in a soft blue sky, we heard of the bombing of Tokyo. It was Tokyo's story: the female announcer, Madame Butterfly, told sadly of how

American planes pursued widows and orphans through the streets, bombing no one and nothing else.

You hear little but the Tokyo radio in these waters. One night we heard Madame Butterfly, another night a silky and highly statistical male. Each program ended with musical selections from a "great composer": Schubert, Mozart, Beethoven, or Bach. No Foster, no Gershwin, no errors.

I mentioned the Sleepwalker to Captain M., in purely friendly terms. The captain was equally friendly.

"I have heard it roll around," he said. "That is probably not one of the big bombs."

The captain, now freighting a load of concentrated hell over hostile waters instead of newsprint out of peaceful ports, had the *D.S.O.* for his previous voyage. He had taken food and equipment into one of the Philippines and brought out refugees. He did not discuss that voyage, nor this one. He looked uneasily at the gunners, the Army kids, who had tossed an empty carton astern and were winging away at it with their machine-guns.

"They shoot an awful lot of bullets," said the captain, frowning against the noise.

He cared less about the prospect of Jap planes than about the company of his dog, a handsome chow named

Ching. Sitting on the watch deck, neat and ascetic, with his white hair rippling slightly in the breeze, the captain played with Ching for hours at a time. He would take off his hornrimmed glasses and put them on the dog's nose and sit back beaming placidly at the spectacle.

I watched the gunners for a while, and saw the red tracer bullets skipping high on the surface of the water, where the target bobbed in our wake. Joe, the mess boy, was sitting on a hatch below, outside the galley. He was reading a Western story called "Lucky Shoe."

"What did you do before you shipped out here, Joe?" I asked him.

"I did a lot of hitch-hiking, around there in Florida and Georgia and the South," Joe said. "There was a funny thing about the way I hitch-hiked, that I never noticed anybody else do. With me, I didn't care where I was going, so long as I was going. If no cars came my way, I crossed the road and hitched the other way. Just so I was going."

You leave Australia, where the food even in the good hotels is only so-so—we'd been in Darwin recently, where the rations were sparse indeed—and come aboard an American freighter, and you enter the promised land. It used to make me hungry just to read about the things to eat that the Pilgrim Fathers piled up at

Thanksgiving time. The *Floating Firecracker* was
Plymouth in spades:

Steak, roast chicken, fricasseed chicken, roast veal
and dressing, ribs of beef, corned shoulder, pork chops
and beans, roast mutton, New England dinner, fish;
potatoes mashed, candied, boiled, and fried; cabbage,
lima beans, cauliflower, beets, turnips, and carrots;
broad plates of rolls, of cheese and cold cuts, of celery
and scallions; platters of a cucumber and onion salad,
floating in dressing, that had no peer; pies, puddings,
cakes, and (once) ice cream; and the standard breakfast of fruit, eggs any style, ham, bacon, potatoes, hot
cakes, toast, honey, syrup, jam, marmalade, milk, and
coffee.

We ate in shifts, in the officers' mess off the captain's
cabin, taking a chair when Joe found room for us. The
lightest eater aboard was the captain. The heaviest—
and the swiftest, silentest, and most ruthless—was the
second engineer.

I walked up to the door of the forward cabin one
day. The second officer and the third officer were playing acey-duecey outside, on the Second's backgammon
board. They said nothing, following me with their eyes,
and a moment later I was inside the door and groping
blindly through acrid fumes that cut up through my
nostrils like knife blades and closed my swimming eyes.

I felt for the doorway and leaped back out on deck. The Third and the Second, when I could see them again, were grinning broadly.

"How do you like it?" said the Second. "They're fumigating in there. Better shut the door."

"It would be a hell of a note," said the Third, shaking the dice, "if he sat on a cargo of bombs and high octane gas this long and then died of rat poison."

The boys were very cheerful.

The *Firecracker* slid through the Coral Sea with her cargo of death for the Japanese. Her crew of Merchant Marine men was getting double pay for the voyage and a bonus for each man besides. This was reminder enough that microscopic pieces of man and ship would fill the air at the first nudge of a Japanese bomb or torpedo. Knowing it, the crew worked placidly, and quarreled those conventional quarrels of men at sea that flame up and die like the flare of a match, and far into the night they argued their immemorial themes: women and money.

The deck engineer had just been married before leaving port. He was wide, squatty, and loud in his love for his new wife, which made him untrue to each in turn of the five women tattooed on his back and chest (including a Red Cross nurse and a mermaid).

"My God, how I love that woman!" the deck engineer would shout in the midst of his work.

The chief engineer, George Smithers, was a genius at the lathe. He took time after lunch to currycomb the ship's rabbit, while the two ship's monkeys from New Zealand stood watch from the rail above. The rabbit, like the crew, had been promised a bonus for the voyage —a mate.

George didn't have to go to sea. He ran a profitable bar for merchant officers in San Francisco, "George's Cave."

"But after I'm ashore awhile I get lousy and sick of liquor," he said, "and I ship out again. I'm in for the duration this time. The joint'll take care of itself."

The *Firecracker* carried two poker games, fore and aft. Forward, in the mess cabin, was the correspondents' game, where Knickerbocker's weakness for raising the size of the pot on two pair kept the rest of us in comfort. Aft was the crew's game, also for table stakes. Here the boatswain suffered and bled and grew more doleful with each day the freighter put behind her.

He, Boats, was a vast pile of muscle and whale fat, with his blue shorts clinging precariously below his hips and his big back burned and scarred from a boiler disaster years before. Boats was losing. With intermittent blasphemies he discussed the peril of using the pound (Australian) as a gambling unit.

"You're used to playing with dollars," said Boats, "and you play with this pound note like it was a buck. You lose three times as much. Hell," said Boats, ciphering rapidly, "you lose three and two-tenths times as much. This Australian cush is gonna make a pauper out of me."

Squalls from the east blew a jet of water over our cots as we slept in the open. The *Firecracker* pitched and grumbled, and the Sleepwalker, the rogue bomb, rolled wakefully to and fro beneath us. Some of the gunners were sick that night—the Army kids who stood watch in shifts at their cherished machine-guns. These were good boys, bright, alert, and a little unlucky, but uncomplaining. Three of them had passed their exams as flying cadets and were passionately interested in planes. The war came just too soon for them: rushed them into vital service protecting our shipping.

"I guess we're here to stay now," said Tommy, slim, dark gunner with Italian blood in his veins. "The Army'll find plenty of new boys at home for the work we were training to do."

The crew, observing everything, did not miss the fact that the gunners had been sick. The crew took it with bland satisfaction. Boats winked as Tommy passed by him to the toilet, white-faced and sheepish. This had been a lucky crew so far, voyaging dangerously but seeing no Japs, and the men were skeptical of the Army and its guns, cluttering up their ship. A moment was coming. . . .

The *Firecracker,* plodding patiently through the milky green sea, was still forty miles off Port Moresby when we saw the mountains of New Guinea against the sky on the port quarter. Patrol planes appeared in the distance, circled us widely, and returned. The gunners craned their necks to identify the planes. The crew, with its goal in sight, took on an extra nonchalance. There were no sharp whistles of relief, no exulting comment—just broader smiles and easier, freer strides about the decks.

We dropped the hook toward dusk. All hands turned out to watch and yell good-by to their five passengers as we swung aboard a launch of the Royal Australian Air Force and chugged away toward the tiny, green, and lovely port of Moresby, toward the copra stores by the jetty, toward the white and yellow deserted houses that sat along the hillside in an arc overlooking the harbor.

Only the captain remained abstracted as he posed

for a last picture with Crotchett's camera and waved his
hand to us above his smooth white head. He still had
to unload those yellow bombs and those big red drums
of high octane gasoline. And the Japs were bombing
Moresby every day.

Post-Log: The bombers and the Zeros came, as
scheduled. The *Firecracker,* unloading, pulled ropes
and tried to flee the harbor. Two Zeros spotted the
gray old coaster and zoomed low for the kill. I did not
see the faces of the crew at that moment, but I know it
was then that Tommy and his gunners, waiting,
squeezed their guns and put a burst into one Zero
while the other swerved away and lit out over the hills.

A little way back in the jungle that afternoon,
Tommy and his mob found the Jap plane they had
gutted, and they came back to the ship with a piece of
wing for a souvenir.

I suspect that the crew and the gunners were a war-
toughened and a friendlier team on the *Firecracker's*
voyage home. I saw the look on the captain's face as he
told us of Tommy's exploit, excited, pleased, and still
a little surprised. He finished his job and sailed away,
and Earle Crotchett, with a sigh of relief, folded his
tripod and removed his camera from the crumbling
veranda above the harbor where he had stood for hour

after hour, not daring to miss the picture he hoped would never come: the *Firecracker* blowing up.

In the days that followed, we saw planes flying off to the north—powered by the fuel, and sowing the bombs, that the *Floating Firecracker* had carried to the men who knew what to do with them.*

* Note 4, page 293.

XVI

Port of Bombs and Butterflies

WE wrote our stories in the upstairs sitting room of a big deserted white house that overlooked the harbor of Port Moresby. The room opened on a rickety wooden balcony from which you could see all of the tiny tropic seaport, and the dark mountains that shouldered the horizon beyond it, and the dusty yellow road that wound inland from the town to the foothills of the Owen Stanley range. Hibiscus and bougainvillea grew tall around the balcony. In the morning, about eight o'clock, Japanese planes would come over Moresby, and the porch made a sort of loge seat commanding not only the target but the skies above it, where the P-40's rose to chase the bombers and dogfight the Zeros.

There was a slit trench by the driveway in front of the house, but we didn't use it because the Japs, bent on wrecking Moresby as an air base, at this time were concentrating their attack on the Allied airdromes and installations farther inland. They never came close to success. When, later, they made their deepest thrust at the town by land, the Allies still held firm control of the air that roofed the line of Japanese march.

There were five of us in the house, counting Crotchett. We were the first of the American press to reach New Guinea, or Papua, as the southeastern segment of the island is properly known. When we finished our stories, we went rattling over miles of coastal bush country in search of censors. The stuff was censored twice there at Moresby, by the RAAF (the Royal Australian Air Force) and the Australian Army, and then at least twice and sometimes three times again when it reached the mainland of Australia. We could speak freely of the country and what was happening there, but in the dateline the name Port Moresby became *"An Advanced Allied Base in the South Pacific"*—a title which, as a matter of fact, told the significance and importance of the little jungle outpost more truly and clearly than any name could do.

Port Moresby, capital of "Papua for the Papuans," is a microscopic metropolis. You could bury and lose it in a few square blocks of downtown New York City. But the tide of the Japanese advance came lapping over Dutch New Guinea, and the north coast of Australian New Guinea, and Timor and other islands to the right and left and, when the enemy was checked at last at the southernmost points of his mighty trespass in the early weeks of 1942, Port Moresby stood in bold relief on the map of the world at war.

It was *the* "advanced Allied base in the South Pacific." It was a knife prodding the belly of the foremost invader. With this weapon, when the Allied retreat stopped short and the Yanks and Australians caught their breath, we began to strike back, stabbing at the new Jap bases of Lae and Salamaua on New Guinea's upper rim and the stronghold of Rabaul, on the island of New Britain, and even farther afield among the airfields and harbors of the Solomon Islands.

That the Jap coveted Moresby from the first, there was never any doubt. He did not mean to stop at Rabaul and Lae. He had found the going easy up till then. His seaborne troops descended upon country that was softened for them by the work of a curious set of fifth columnists: men of German stock posing as missionaries, who rode among the native villages of northern New Guinea and taught the natives, among other things, to greet them with the Nazi salute. These spreaders of the Word were ready for the coming of the Japanese. Their pupils cooperated with the invader as guides and workers in country even tougher and more tangled than Malaya or Bataan. Over Rabaul, capital and chief city of the Mandated Territory of New Guinea, Australia's little Wirraway fighter plane was too slow and flimsy a job to challenge the enemy's bombers and his transports.

The Japs, eyes cocked on the lonely salient of Moresby, plunged onward, overland. It was the rainy season. Swollen rivers and wild, sodden mountains turned them back. So they abandoned the direct route across New Guinea and tried by sea. General MacArthur has since revealed what the Allied Command felt sure of from the beginning: that the Jap armada in the Coral Sea in May was bound for Moresby, to pinch off our menacing outpost and consolidate Jap holdings north of Australia. Once more the enemy failed. Our planes smashed his fleet and dealt him his first important defeat of the war.

His third try was by land again: this time at the point where the island's neck stretches thinnest, with snipers and jungle troops trained and camouflaged for the style of fighting that overran British and American lines in the early campaigns of the Pacific. I remember Colonel Edward Thomas Brennan talking about the possibilities of this sort of attack back in April. Brennan, a big, convivial Australian doctor, was chief medical officer of the forces at Port Moresby and before that was the public health administrator of the New Guinea territory. He had sailed the surrounding waters and tramped the country and doctored its people for years. He was our tireless guide in the Moresby region. I doubt if any white man on the island knew its history, customs, and half-charted terrain better than he.

"It's a temptation," said the colonel one day, as his car panted up the jungle "road" or track that led, dwindling as it went, from the coastal plain into the mountains back of Moresby, "to say that no large armed force can cross New Guinea by land. You see what the country is like. But men have done it before, whites as well as natives, and I suppose that men can do it again."

He was right, and the Japs were the first to prove it, with their neatly planned push from the Gona-Buna base, just across the island's neck. They came down to Kokoda, on the north side of the Owen Stanleys, and paused there to expand the new outpost and improve their line of communications. Then they forced the only true gap through the mountains and fanned outward to filter toward the plain that surrounds Port Moresby. The towns by which the Allied Command defined the Jap advance—you may have read their names: Menari, Ioridaiwa, Wairopi, Efogi—were never more than fetid clusters of native huts in the thick green wilderness. Jap snipers sifted forward from tree to tree along the trail, their faces and uniforms stained green or a mottle of brown and green. They veered from the track from time to time, penetrating growth that seemed to defy armed troops, to take the Australian outposts in flank.

They might have had Moresby in September, 1942, but for two factors: Allied control of the air, from which we plastered their supply line and bases with bombs and treetop machine-gun fire; and the swiftness with which Australia's Diggers mastered this new art of war and counter-attacked.

In short, the garrison was prepared, even though most of the officers and men I spoke with in the spring were skeptical of the possibilities of a land attack. If the Japs did attempt and carry off this feat of crossing New Guinea in force, paving the way for the subsequent Allied advance by the same trail, it was probably because of the strength of their motive.

"I think we and the Nips are agreed," Brennan had said, "that the stake is worth it."

The stake was Port Moresby. The little town is in the southeast corner of the Gulf of Papua, a broad knuckle of the Coral Sea. It was a doleful navigator who baptized those waters, for Moresby's harbor is flanked right and left in the coastline by Bootless Inlet and Caution Bay.

I first saw the town from the sea. It lies along the back curve of a beautiful little jughandle harbor, white and yellow houses and stores and government buildings clustered among low green hills that survey the harbor like the tiers of an amphitheater. Back of the hills is a dusty plain rising steadily to the mountains that wall the interior. Some of these mountains, like Albert Edward and Victoria (also called Mount Owen Stanley), are twelve to thirteen thousand feet high. Jap raiders flying between the two big peaks needed at least nine thousand feet of altitude as they came in.

The air is clear in the mountains, and the land rich and green, but Moresby itself sits at the edge of the coastal lowland, twenty-five miles broad, and there the air is steaming and heavy even in the dry season, and the sun burns wickedly. It is fever country. Among the troops the fever rate never exceeded one percent at a given time, but few men stay there long without collecting their ration of dengue or malaria.

Moresby's mosquitoes are as notorious as the wolves of the steppes. We hadn't been in town an hour before a Digger brought us abreast of the situation with mosquito gag 1A:

"The way the mosquitoes are in this place, Yank, they reach in your pocket, look up your blood type in your papers, and then send for their friends."

When we set up housekeeping, with our five cots placed in a row, we always spread mosquito nets over the cots at night. But you have to be an engineering genius, like Crotchett, the newsreel man, to defy the Moresby mosquitoes with nets. Earle had his bed rigged as tightly and handsomely and complexly as a three-master under full sail. They never got to him. They murdered your correspondent. This was chiefly because I was a punk technician with a net, but I like to think also that the mosquitoes who favored our place for their evening snack looked upon me as the blue plate special.

The town was bright in the sun but nearly deserted when we came ashore in a cutter the first afternoon of our stay in Port Moresby. Empty shipping offices and stores lined the waterfront, centering about the local compound and copra store of the Burns-Philp Company, a far-flung merchant and trading house with peacetime agencies all over the south seas. Farther up the hill, in the center of town, were two hotels, the Moresby and the Papua. As capital of the Papuan Territory, Moresby did have certain claims to metropolitan standing, and the hotels were small but trig and shiny. They were completely vacant now. So were the "main streets" of dirt and loose stone, and the white houses, many with windows broken from the concussion of Jap bombs that fell near the harbor. The town had been evacuated by military order. The order extended even to government offices, and this gave us our chance to exercise squatters' right in the long disheveled house of stucco and fibroid that once lodged the Ministry of Interior—the house with the broken balcony, perched on a shelf of hillside a couple of hundred yards above the docks.

On these docks we saw scattered groups of the natives of Papua. They were workers, assigned to special jobs on the waterfront. The Papuan native, unlike the Aboriginal of Australia, is intelligent and a fine physical specimen. He speaks the soft, mellifluous tongue called Motuan, stemming from none of the standard language stocks of the Pacific islands. In some cases, where he has come under missionary influence, he speaks good English; good enough to embarrass your correspondent, who plunged into some peculiar variety of pidgin when accosted by a young native boy on the road, and was gently rebuked for his pains.

"Where do you come from?" said the native.

"Oh, very far place, America," mumbled your correspondent, with gestures designed to enlighten the primitive mind.

"The United States?" said the boy quietly. "Yes, that is a great distance from here."

He, like many of the other younger native men, was a camp-servant for the Moresby garrison. Shortly after we moved into the white house, the Australian commander sent Ronnie, Johnny, Beaverbrook, and George to us, four boys who had stolen rice and were delegated to us Yanks as a penalty for their crime. Three of them wore white hibiscus blossoms in their high black hair,

and the fourth wore a crimson comb. They materialized like genii, and were standing in a circle around
Crotchett, watching him mend a camera, when I saw
them for the first and last time. The newsreel man
waved nonchalantly at the visitors.

"They stole chickens," he said.

"Rice," corrected Beaverbrook, their spokesman,
spurning the old Tennessee tradition in which Crotchett had tried to involve him.

"All right, rice," said Crotchett. "So they have to
work for us."

Ronnie, Johnny, Beaverbrook, and George shrugged
their shoulders in unison and looked meaningly at a
corner of the room where Knickerbocker had piled the
tinned pears and tinned beans he carried around as a
challenge to the perils of darkest New Guinea. I gave
them each a can. Then I sat down at my typewriter
and started to work. Beaverbrook, reading over my
shoulder, summoned the other three, and they stood
together behind me commenting freely in Motuan. I
did not like the tone of their voices.

"We will do the laundry," announced Beaverbrook
pretty soon.

"Fine," I said enthusiastically.

"Where is the soap?"

We didn't have any soap.

"Where is the water?"

Water ran from our taps and showers at exactly four o'clock in the morning, for about two minutes, at which time you could bathe and flush a toilet if you acted fast. Now and then a scout would report signs of H_2O in the starboard faucet at 7 A.M., but by the time the rest of us had rushed to the scene in answer to his wild alarm, the water was gone and the situation was back to normal. Crotchett outlined this scenario to Ronnie, Johnny, Beaverbrook, and George. They thought it over.

"Good-by," said Beaverbrook, and the four boys filed down the stairway and out of our lives. There was no way of telling whether they were resolved to be better citizens in the future or not.

Papua is flowery country, and the air is full of butterflies and the cries of strange birds. The natives, with their bright-colored *ramis*—sarongs—and the flowers in their hair, blend with a lush and poetic background that seems to swallow up war and its traces. We found, however, when we penetrated the bush to a seaside village near Moresby, that Papuans had taken cognizance of the Jap and his bombs and our own anti-aircraft shells. They were moving inland, lock, stock, and barrel. Only a dozen were left. One of these was a headman, or Boss, who accepted a cigarette when he received us and clamped it between ancient teeth that were stained scarlet with betel nut juice.

The village stood on stilts, on the beach. It was approached from the land side by a crude causeway of loose boulders and logs spanning a tidal marsh. The Boss met us at the end of the causeway, in the shadow of a long shack of thatched bark and leaves that was somewhat better built than the rest—the missionary school. The natives he introduced us to all spoke fair English. One was a girl of nineteen, who giggled when Crotchett asked her to pose for pictures; but posed just the same, with great poise and assurance. She would have been attractive but for the sad partiality to betel nut she shared with all the villagers. The juice made ragged red gashes of their mouths. Some of the men dyed their hair with it, turning the black kinks to yellow red.

The Boss chewed his cigarette and said that he and his people did not care for airplanes.

"One fell on the hill there," he said, pointing to a knob of ground near by.

"A Jap?"

"Yes, red ball. They took it away. Too close," said the decrepit sachem, and waved a hand toward the jungle back of the village. "We all go that way tomorrow. Rest gone yesterday."

Leaving there, we met native constables on the road who confirmed this account.

"All villages near Port Moresby will be empty soon,"

said one of them. The New Guinea constabulary is recruited from the strongest and smartest natives, the best trackers and marksmen. Two of its members stood guard day and night over the headquarters of the Australian commander. Keepers of the peace in peacetime, agents of the civil government, they were more valuable in war as scouts and sentinels. Some of them maintained liaison between headquarters and a group of mysterious, seldom-mentioned guerilla operatives who ranged far inland, as far as the Japanese outposts, and were known as the *N.G.V.R.*—the New Guinea Volunteer Rifles.

Papua in peacetime was governed by the policy "Papua for the Papuans," which meant that commercial exploitation was discouraged and the natives left largely to their natural devices. This made it a sort of poor relation to the Mandated Territory of New Guinea to the north. The Mandated Territory, with Rabaul for a capital, coined its own money and had its own administration of customs, public health, and revenue, distinct from the Australian government on the mainland. Its silver coins were made with holes in them, so that the natives, having no pockets, might carry them on strings around their necks. The Mandate sometimes showed a profit of forty or fifty thousand pounds a year. Papua, on the other hand, was a primitive ward of Australia and strictly on the cuff. All this has been changed in the last year or two—by Japan, with guns, and by Australia, with pen and paper. Unification of the Mandate and Papua, launched before the war, has been carried through—on paper. The commander in Port Moresby during our stay was the governor of all of Australian New Guinea and New Britain, and his "seat" was far-off Rabaul: a cool dismissal of the fact that Rabaul literally crawled with Japs and the fiat paper money they take with them everywhere.

White men had long wished to exploit Papua's rubber, but the "primitive" policy of pre-war days was against it, and only a few plantations existed in the rich wilderness. We visited one of these one day with Colonel Brennan, driving up the winding, rutted road to the cool, clear of the mountain shelves.

Jap bombers came over before we left the plain and the airfields behind us. We climbed out of the car and took cover in long grass at the edge of a drome. The enemy's shooting was usually pretty good until our fighters could climb up and chase him off. We saw one heavy bomb dig a crater a hundred yards away. When it was over we got back in the car and labored on up the mountain track through the foothills of the Owen Stanleys. A foaming brown stream, the Laloki, skirted the road. It fell to the plain in sheer falls five hundred feet high. The jungle around us was low, thick growth, brilliant with flowers and butterflies. The colonel extended good will to friends of his at posts along the way, from a big square silver flask that locked and unlocked with a key and made him the envy of the region.

The plantation, when we found it, was an oasis of smooth British greenery in the tanglewood. Time stood still here, and the only signs of war the field hands saw were planes high overhead flying to and from Port Moresby. We drove up to the manor house through lawns and gardens. White overseers and native hands were playing cricket on a stretch of turf, and the natives were beating hell out of the whites. There was a golf course around the house, with rough putting greens staked off in squares—all this only twenty-five air miles from a focal point of the South Pacific's hottest war zone.

We had lunch with the chief overseer. A Papuan child no more than three feet high passed cold ham and chicken and preserves around the table.

The plantation produced a million pounds of rubber a year in peacetime, and is ordinarily worked by four hundred and fifty natives, whose head boys, to the number of thirty, are allowed to keep their wives on the place. The other hands work out a two-year contract and then go back to their villages in the bush to buy wives with the money they have earned. Eight pounds will buy a wife, so will two pigs; the pig being a valued character in those parts and generally preferred to children. A wife is bought on approval. If she turns out to be a poor worker, her husband can obtain government permission to return her to her father and get his money back.

Pigs, axes, and spears are units of currency, as well as money. Pigs are housebroken and practically members of the family until the time comes to translate them into pork chops. A family procession walking through the bush is apt to consist of husband first, wife second, pig third, and a domesticated cassowary bringing up the rear. The cassowary is also a great family friend until he graduates from this life and becomes fricassee.

As for cannibalism among the New Guinea natives, it is highly selective and a more or less isolated gesture in the ritual of revenge. If, on killing a citizen of another village by way of evening a score, the members of a certain tribe become so emotionally stirred as to eat him, the victim's kinsmen are likely to reply in kind at the first opportunity. But anthropophagy for its own sake almost never occurs.

It was on the night that followed our trip into the mountains, as I recall, that our driver, a Digger whom we came to know as Sorrowful Hunt, threw our little road company into a state of alarm by bursting into

tears as he pulled the car up in front of the old home-
stead on the hill. We rallied around Hunt, patting him
anxiously on the back and asking what was wrong.

"I am a free-born soldier," sobbed the driver, who
was also a heavyweight wrestler to all appearances. He
would say nothing more for some time.

It developed eventually that in paying a call at headquarters on the way home we had left Hunt waiting
outside in the car too long. There was some merit in
his charge, and we sprinted around in a state of great
embarrassment looking for peace-offerings, such as car-
tons of cigarettes, to ply him with. In the end, Sorrowful Hunt dried his tears and agreed to let bygones be
bygones. But he had the upper hand of us from there
on. Though he did not weep again, he let it be felt that
he might, at any time. This threat put him in a position of power which he never relinquished.

The Moresby garrison, as far as land troops were
concerned, was then almost entirely Australian. These
Diggers, gradually reinforced by seasoned comrades
from the Middle East, were the ones who ambushed the
Japanese at Milne Bay, at Papua's eastern tip, in August, 1942, and chased the enemy's vanguard and snipers
back across the mountains from the Moresby plain in
September. Few of them, certainly not the desert soldiers, had ever seen terrain as wildly wicked as the

mountain jungle of New Guinea, but they were rugged fighters, and learned new tricks quickly.*

The only American ground troops in Moresby, in the spring, were Negro stevedore outfits drawn from the South and Middle West of the United States. They were there to develop the airfields and rack up the metal-based runways from which the Allied flyers plastered Lae and Salamaua and Rabaul. I saw the first of them on the day of their arrival in Moresby, in the midst of their first air raid alarm.

The troops were inspecting the town when the siren wailed, and they came tumbling out of the deserted Hotel Moresby into the white noon heat and made for the slit trenches, as ordered. There they shouted cheerfully back and forth across the dusty road to one another. A big brown private first class saw me and called out:

"How do they shoot, pretty good?"

"Just fair."

"Good, that's fine," he said, and turned to a neighbor in his trench. "Man here," he reported, jerking a thumb in my direction, "says they can't even find the right county."

From across the road another voice boomed out in the dusty tropic sunlight—"It's a long way from East St. Louis!"

* Note 5, page 294.

Port Moresby, in fact, by peacetime standards, was as far away from anywhere as anyone could get. War, which adjusts the world to its own rules and its own design, put red letters on the map against the site of a sleepy, infinitesimal jungle port that not more than one American in one hundred thousand ever heard of before Pearl Harbor.

XVII

Between Zeros

WHEN the sun sank behind the hills west of Port
Moresby, native boys pulled blackout curtains over the
windows of the RAAF clubhouse, and there, by dim
light, the flyers of Australia and their American teammates relaxed at the bar, sang songs, played the phonograph, read their letters, turned the leaves of such
newspapers and magazines as reached the Papuan outpost, and talked.

Their talk was shaped by certain unwritten rules.
Australians of the air force are far closer to England
than the soldiers of the Army, and the clubhouse at
Moresby, a long, rectangular, one-story shack some
little distance from the town, was the most British
corner of the garrison. Many of the airmen had flown
with the RAF over England and the Channel and the
European continent in the first two years of the war,
before the safety of Australia was directly involved.
Then they came home to fight, but they did not forget
England. The war of Englishmen, Frenchmen, Norse-
men, and Germans, so remote from the average Aus-

tralian at home, was fresh in the minds of these flyers. They flew P-40's and P-39's now, but they had flown Spitfires and Hurricanes. They had known the Messerschmitt before they saw the Zero. Along with the Anzac troops from the African desert, they were the first veterans of "two" wars—of both wings of the global war.

Their toasts were English, and the things they said and the things they did not say. The Americans who were stationed beside them in Moresby and came to the RAAF bar—the "Oasis"—in the evening quickly fell in with these ways. The difference between Americans and British in this matter of heroic reticence is only one of form, anyhow. If the Yanks are inclined to betray a little more relish in a good day's fighting, and to do so a little more noisily, they are still firmly bound by school and college traditions that make it next to criminal to parade your feats of valor, your wealth, or your social successes.

Flyers and collegians have much the same frozen notion about what constitutes muckerism. For the flyer, too, there is a deeper consideration. He lived today. He may die tomorrow. All his instinct is to shun the sort of shop talk that involves himself and his deeds personally.

The Moresby flyers met the Jap every day. You drank with men at the Oasis one night who were not there the next. No notice was taken of this, in a place so public as the clubhouse. It was a rare happening when Wing Commander Pearce, the RAAF's ranking officer in Port Moresby at the time, spoke of the death of John Jackson, Squadron Leader Jackson, whom I mentioned earlier. He did so only in answer to a question one of us asked.

"I shouldn't have let him go up," said Pearce. "He was too old for this work."

Pearce said nothing more about it. His rigid policy was to keep his emotions and the problems of his command to himself. Jackson's younger brother, who brought down three Zeros in one afternoon a few days later, said nothing about it at all. The standard tone of talk in the RAAF bar, social talk, as apart from command business, was insulting—the cool and stylized banter of "well-bred" Britons everywhere. The Australian flyers, under strong British influence, merely added a few twists of their own. The Yanks, as I started to say, were perfectly familiar with the tune. Only the lyrics were different.

In spite of the international pact of reticence, however, the Oasis was by way of being a clearing-house of information on the course of the war in New Guinea. It was there, after dark, that you got the day's score, and a few terse details of the fighting. It was there I heard of the four bags of mail from Australian prisoners in Rabaul that the Japs dropped over Moresby one morning, and saw the accompanying note from "the Japanese Headquarters" as it passed from hand to hand at the bar; there that we checked the facts in our stories, before they were read by Lieutenant Ivor McIvor, the tall, thin, and owlish young man who served as censor for the RAAF.

We heard arguments about rival brands of planes there, and got wind of some of the local prejudices: most of the Australians at the time held out hotly for the B-25's and B-26's, American medium bombers, over the B-17 or Flying Fortress. I mention this to show how completely judgment in matters of this sort is controlled by local conditions and local observations; also to emphasize that once a plane—the P-40 say, or the B-17—has been corrected in action and brought to something near its best level of performance, ninety per cent of the arguments it stirs up among flyers grow from the fact that the plane does not meet every purpose in the book. No plane does.

Pearce, McIvor, and others who served in England had seen the early Flying Fortress that was, among other weaknesses, insufficiently gunned. That was the same Fortress that first appeared in the Pacific. Later, armed from teeth to tail, the B-17 could use its range to rain hell on Rabaul with better effect than the B-25's and B-26's—which nevertheless earned the admiration of the Australians in New Guinea, the one by its steadiness, the other by its speed, in the lashing of Lae and Salamaua. The 26 could outrun the fastest Zero built by fifty miles an hour.

They spoke of planes, all right, at the Oasis and at the mess shack across the road, even if they did not speak of what they did in them and what had happened today and what would happen tomorrow.

When the radio in one corner of the clubhouse was turned on for a news broadcast, there were seldom more than half a dozen men gathered around it to listen. The rest ignored it for their drinks and their magazines and their talk. Wing Commander Dick Cohen, veteran of the Battle of Britain, remembered the night spots, bands, and books he had liked best in a brief furlough in New York. That was the sort of stuff that roused the RAAF bar to its highest state of animation.

You could get beer at the bar at all times and whisky when it happened to be in stock, and the ice generally lasted long enough to supply all but the late stayers. Next to beer, the favorite hot-weather drink—and Port Moresby has never seen a cool day or night—was gin mixed with lime juice. The wassail flourished in an atmosphere that was blended of tensity and tropical heat and the half-light of the dimout.

Pearce gave a *shivoo,* or party, one night for Cohen,

his comrade-in-arms, who was headed home to take
over an organization job. There was a storm outside,
and the torrential Papuan rain drove down on the
shack and seemed to shake it on its flimsy foundation.
Visitors who had found the Oasis before the deluge
broke immediately became guests, if not speakers.
Each speaker in turn—and practically everyone spoke,
from Big Mike, the transport pilot, who happened to
be in port that night, to Angus, the dour custodian
of the cellar—was hoisted upon the bar and greeted
with a ritual of songs, which began with:

> "Why was he born so beautiful,
> Why was he born so beautiful,
> Why was he born so beautiful,
> Why was he born at all?"

The Yanks in the audience joined in the chants as
fast as they learned them, down to the one which
spurned any effort by any orator to become solemn, to
the tune of *Bring Back my Bonnie to me:*

> "It all sounds like ———— to me, to me,
> It all sounds like ———— to me!"

And in the background, with the detachment and
singlemindedness which airmen seem to possess beyond all other soldiers, one group of pilots discussed

tarpon-fishing while two other non-revelers at a table
off in a corner collaborated on a month-old crossword
puzzle, heedless of the songs and shouts and the roaring rush of the rain.

When Buzz Wagner came through the Oasis, bound
to or from the Jap country to the north, the song of
the evening was one with a dozen or more verses,
adapted by Yankee flyers from Walt Disney's *Pinocchio*,
with the chorus:

> "Hey, diddle-de-dee,
> A pilot's life for me!"

The courteous Australians of the RAAF did not
know quite what to make of Wagner at first. They
were told a "Colonel Wagner" would pass that way
to confer with them on the needs and problems of
American pursuit flyers in the area. His fame preceded
him; no man in the Pacific had shot down so many
Japs. What they saw, when he walked into the clubhouse one evening, was a slim, hatless youth in a cover-
all flying suit, who looked about twenty years old
and was only five years older. Wagner at the time was
developing his new black mustache, with dignity. He
stood alone near the bar a few minutes before Wing
Commander Pearce, reconciling the stranger's youth
with the silver oak-leaves of lieutenant-colonelcy on his

shoulders, swallowed his surprise and stepped forward gravely to negotiate.

If Wagner carried any clue about him to his career as a Jap-killer, it was in his eyes, as cool and deadly a pair of eyes as you would wish to see. A few days later, in his début over New Guinea, he brought down a probable six Zeros in a single flight.

It was the crossroads quality of the RAAF club at Port Moresby—the fact that famous characters of many nations appeared there, suddenly and informally, to pass the time of day or night—which set it apart from its prototypes in England and other air-battle zones; that and the jungle flavor of the country. Instead of English batmen and campservants, there were the dark boys of Papua, with their white or crimson *ramis* and flowers in their hair, waiting on table at mess, sweeping the floors, carrying ice and supplies to the bar, changing records on the phonograph. The kid who handled the music-box, if nobody made a special request, played his own two favorite records alternately and steadily: "Margie" and "Franklin D. Roosevelt Jones." These, being good tunes, sounded as well in the hot black New Guinea night as anywhere else.

The Japs seldom raided Moresby by dark, but now and then there was a night alarm, false or otherwise. When it sounded, the airmen filed rapidly out of doors into the shadows and took cover among the fields and hills around the shack, in slit trenches, like any civilian or ground soldier. Their judgment of what might be coming was sounder technically than the groundling's, but their attitude toward what might be dropped from above was no bolder. I've heard it said that flyers on the ground during an air raid are inclined to be more jittery than other men. I've never noticed any marked difference, but if the argument is true, it is also understandable. The habit of being bombed is the greatest builder of nonchalance toward bombing. Active airmen, nine times out of ten, are up in the air fighting when the bombs fall.

The tempo of war in New Guinea grew faster in the summer months that followed our expedition there. MacArthur and his Australian lieutenants sent up the best troops they could muster, airmen as well as infantry and artillery, and the Oasis was stampeded by the flower of American and Australian flying men. Squadron Leader Keith Truscott—"Bluey" Truscott—passed through, fresh from feats at Milne Bay that transcended the work in England which made him the aerial darling of his native Melbourne and most of the rest of Australia as well.

I mention Truscott, whom I met in Melbourne, because he had characteristics that were absolutely certain to qualify him as a hero for Australia, given his record in the sky. Bluey was an athlete. Born of humble working people in the capital of Australian football, he was one of the country's best professional players by the time he reached his late 'teens. He was redhaired, of middle height, wide as a tram car, inclined to be rolypoly, and possessed of an ineradicable grin.

All this made him the people's choice, when he joined the RAF in England as a Spitfire pilot, and Bluey did the rest. He was the sidekick or cobber of England's own favorite pursuit ace, the Irishman, Paddy Finucane, who later fell to his death in the Channel. Bluey shared in the glory of the Finucane squadron and ran his personal toll of Heinkels and Messerschmitts well into two figures. Every move he made was relayed to the press at home, though I gathered from gentlemen on the football beat in the State of Victoria that Bluey's air victories enchanted the public no more than certain of his passages on the ground—as when, watching a pick-up rugby game, he suddenly kicked the ball with the virtuosity that only Australians possess, and astounded every Englishman within ten miles.

"When Bluey showed 'em how," a newspaper football critic told me, "it tickled the folks at home."

Bluey had just returned from England when I first met him. He accepted an invitation from his old team, Melbourne, to play football against Richmond on a

Saturday afternoon—a little recklessly, since he also accepted the hospitality of practically all his admirers, consisting of champagne, on Friday night. I saw the ball game. K. Truscott started and finished, as advertised. He got a sort of submarine view of the match, as the thundering herd rolled back and forth over his prostrate form, but he took the mud bath cheerfully and the crowd's ovation with modest grace.

A slight civic and military contretemps developed after the game, when a wealthy sportsman identified with what we call "rackets" sent Bluey a check for a large number of pounds, to be shared with Paddy Finucane. It caused much excitement along the boulevards, till Bluey's advisers recalled an RAF rule against this sort of thing and counseled him to give back the check.

The Yanks in New Guinea knew how the wealthy sportsman felt, when they saw what Bluey could do with a plane. They, too, members of an anti-aircraft outfit that fought at Milne Bay, made him a gift, this time of clothing, and sent a letter with it which cited the work of the Australian fighter squadrons in this defeat of the Japanese: "You all deserve more praise than you will ever receive."

It was the first overt compliment paid by American troops to Australian armed forces. Truscott alone, in the Milne Bay action, sank six enemy invasion barges

and wiped out a column of fifty Japs with his machine
guns. The switch from the Spitfire to the P-40, which
all Australian fighter pilots had to make who came
home from England, apparently did not inconvenience
Bluey in the least; nor the switch from German targets
to Japanese.*

Truscott's case indicates that birth and wealth have
nothing to do with the fact that the air force constitutes a sort of aristocracy of war among the Australians. The RAAF eats better, drinks better, dresses
better—and the rest of the troops, for all their fanatically democratic attitude toward army life and the
world in general, accept this. The whole country takes
a special pride in its airmen that has been felt for no
other force of Australian soldiers since the campaign
of Gallipoli.

The subalterns of the RAAF had steaks and chops
at mess; the general commanding the port, up the road
among his infantry and artillery, did no better than
tinned beef and custard. Nor did the general have anything to match the Oasis.

The men of the RAAF were a buying crowd, in
their bar; though they did not "buy" drinks for their
guests, they "shouted," to the slight confusion of Allen
Raymond. Raymond started to pay for his grog once.
A Squadron Leader laid a hand on his arm.

* Note 6, page 294.

"I'm shouting," he said.

"Don't mention it," said Raymond dreamily. He pushed the money across the bar.

"It's my shout," protested the Australian, hurt. "But of course, if you don't want..."

"You shout, I'll drink," said the delegate of the *New York Herald Tribune*, deep in his revery, and it took some time to bring these two proud minds into a common understanding of the situation.

XVIII

Seven Deadly Young Men

"AVIATION METEOROLOGICAL REPORT: for the air
route from —— to Lae. Layer of cloud over south side
of ranges at 7/9000 ft. Broken patches cloud between
2,000 and 15,000 ft. on north side. Broken cloud 3/5000
ft. over target. Winds light and variable all levels."

Communiqué from General MacArthur's Headquarters: "New Guinea—Lae: In a brilliant attack our
air force bombed and machine-gunned the airdrome
heavily. Many direct hits were scored on a line of thirty
planes. Large fires were observed in the target area."

In between those terse reports, preface and epilogue,
came the finest hayride I ever took. It was a voyage of
exploration, a voyage of discovery, a fight, a picnic, and
a ringside view of the enemy being lathered. More than
that, though, and stripped of gaudy trappings: it was a
revelation of how deadly seven young, cheerful American men can be when they are teamed together in

the execution of a stroke of war they have studied and mastered.

Northern Australia and Papua were a slingshot, from which we catapulted planes with bombs to scatter Japanese concentrations, to smash Jap bases, ships, and aircraft, to harry Tojo and keep him hopping—and to beat a path for the day when America and Australia would strike north in balanced force to win back the islands of the Pacific.

At first these were not giant raids on the scale of Cologne and Hamburg. They were neat, sharp, trim raids. Our medium bombers carried the ball—two-engined jobs, the steady-going B-25 that Jimmy Doolittle took to Tokyo and the fast, hot B-26. They had some help from a bigger bomber, but the scale of the work suited the 25's and 26's, and they won the hearts of the Australians who flew and worked alongside and of our crews themselves.

The pilot sitting beside me showed his teeth exultantly as we rode home from the blistering of Lae.

"I'm impartial," he lied at the top of his voice. "But that's the best plane in the world."

Whether it was or not, it was the plane he was learning and loving his job in, the job in this war that Americans and Britons are developing with fullest genius: the smiting of the enemy from the air.

I met the crew in front of the plane, a heavy shadow

lined up with other shadows on the field in the early
morning darkness. The men were standing in a knot,
chewing cheese and crackers. They offered me some.
Then the pilot, full of good will, dug me a piece of
fruit cake out of a box. He wore a white mosquito
head-net cocked rakishly over his nose, and he was taut
and boisterous and strictly business all at the same
time.

A gunner from another plane walked over and
traded limericks with our bombardier. The pilot stood
and listened detachedly, gnawing fruit cake.

He was Lieutenant Robert R. Hatch, from Golds-
boro, North Carolina, with a wide puckish face and a
shrewd eye. He was the captain of this team—and I
tell you the home towns because there is no better
way of describing how all of America, plain, mountain,
lake town, river town, seaport, manufacturing town,
is assimilated by the work of sowing death in far corners of the earth:

Co-pilot: Lieutenant Duncan A. Seffern, Manawa,
Wisconsin, tall, thin, a kidder and a baseball fan, culti-
vating abortive whiskers on his upper lip.

Navigator: Lieutenant John R. Bevan, Boston, thick-
set and big-shouldered, once a football player at Wes-
leyan.

Bombardier: Corporal Leroy Ware, Navasota, Texas,

sandy-haired and smiling—"best bombardier in the business," says Hatch with captainly pride.

Radio operator: Corporal Leonard G. Robinson, Wellsville, Missouri, towheaded, handsome kid with the worldly nonchalance and vocabulary of a Bing Crosby.

Turret gunner: Private First Class James F. Shemberger, South Bend, Indiana, strong-handed, affable, an automobile worker before the war.

Engineer and tail gunner: Private First Class Richard I. Slater, Watkins Glen, New York, dark, slim, good-looking, quick at repartee.

"Let's go!" said Hatch, catching the signal.

I crawled into the belly of the plane, to find the navigator busy at work. The men took their places. We had rushed down the runway in our turn, and were rocketing toward our goal on the north coast of New Guinea before I observed the extra passenger. A small frog jumped across the radio operator's table and vanished under the navigator's desk. I didn't see him again, but for better or worse he was with us when Lae was bombed.

We were past Papua and past the mountains when the sun came up. Shaped like the profile of a turtle headed west in a hurry, the island of New Guinea presented the hump of its shell to us as we moved high over the coastline, hung briefly over the fifth degree of south latitude, and then swung back toward the target.

The plane was on top of Lae before I discovered it firsthand, tucked in a cleft of coastline, behind a round little harbor. We swept down in a clean angle, as though we were riding a shaft of the rising sun. I saw Hatch's left arm go up in a fierce, triumphant gesture, and looking over his shoulder I saw planes, fat planes, lined up on the square-cut field below.

It came fast then. We hit them from 1,200 feet.

Turning back quickly, I peered down the well of the bomb bay, with Bevan. The shutters flew open beneath us, and we watched the long, sleek yellow pineapples fall clear and hurtle down on the field. They smashed cleanly on the target, all of them, with a concussion that shook the plane in the air and made us flinch away from the hole. We saw fires breaking out before the shutters closed. Then we were climbing.

Say what you will about the Zero, this Jap pursuit plane with the red ball on its dingy green fuselage is ubiquitous, and when it finds you it fawns upon you like a puppy with machine guns for a tongue. Antiaircraft burst around us, and rocked us, but the airman seldom worries about those long-shot gamblers on the ground. More sinister were the red lines that cut across our nose: tracer bullets. A Zero was alongside.

He wasn't with us long. Shemberger threw a burst back at him from the turret, and then we went away from him as though he were anchored—which is the way it seems when you have an advantage of more than sixty miles an hour in speed, as we did. No Zero lived at that time that could catch the ship we rode.

The bomber's job is done when she drops her load, and no bomber lingers around to duck-shoot at Zeros for the hell of it. We moved rapidly out of there, and when we were well out the ebullient Hatch turned over the controls to Seffern and came back whooping and yelling congratulations to his team over the roar of the engines.

"Best raid I been on!" he shouted. "They all fell and they all hit."

Ware, from the bombardier's nest, followed him back with a grin that almost split his face in two. Hatch hugged him, and Ware, beaming, looked down at his thumb and began to suck it. There was a fresh cut there he hadn't noticed till now. Still beaming, he bandaged the cut.

"That's the kind of shot I like to get at 'em," he bawled out. "Couldn't miss."

Big Bevan, who had led us unerringly to the target over the sea and mountains, nodded solemnly. Robbie, the operator, slapped Ware on the shoulder and went back to his radio. We had company by now; the kind we liked. Other planes of our flight were to left and right and dead ahead of us, talking the morning's work back and forth on the radio.

Exhilaration filled the ship all the way south across the mountains and over the green Coral Sea, where the atolls made yellow blisters on the surface below us and Hatch let me take the controls for a minute and shook with laughter when we promptly lost altitude.

"Say," yelled the pilot presently, "did you notice you got no parachute on? We didn't have an extra one. But it don't make any difference."

"It don't?"

"No. Our policy is to all go down with the ship. That way, we land together and we all got a chance together."

We stopped to gas up at a barren little base on the way home. There was bread and marmalade at the mess shack there, and oranges. Waiting on the field, Hatch and Seffern played catch with an orange, and Seffern, as he wound up elaborately, told of the only home run he ever hit in his life. Young Robbie spoke to me tolerantly of the fourth estate—"Good, clean work," he pronounced. Bevan, the Boston athlete, wanted to know how the Bruins had made out in the last Stanley Cup hockey playoffs. They hadn't made out so good.

We got our last thrill of the day then, thrown in for

good measure and absolutely unsolicited. Doggedly the Zeros had trailed us south, and with them came bombers. The alarm sounded, and the crews on the ground beelined for their planes, for there is nothing more humiliating, useless, and downright impractical than to be caught on the ground, in the open, with your aeronautical pants down.

There is nothing more scary, I should add, because something always goes a little wrong when you try to take off under the condition known as "or else." One of the engines missed. Then the door failed to shut tight, and Ware had to leap down to the ground again to adjust it from the outside. But we did get off, after sitting there for what seemed like a couple of minutes longer than forever. For one of the ships in our flight, it was closer than a barbershop shave—the first of the Mitsubishis to arrive, dropped a bomb near by that damaged our neighbor's fuselage.

But we all got home. All the teams that went north to plaster Lae that day in behalf of democracy came safely to roost at their base. It was there that Hatch proudly showed me his ship's bullet scars from her last mission—"we got a square hit on an aircraft carrier"—and it was there, as we waited for the truck to take us to mess, that the northerners in the crew considered ways and means to mutiny against Hatch; he had painted the name "Dixie" on her nose over her trade mark of the Jap carrier going down.

At mess the chef piled the hamburgers and mashed potatoes high on the table in front of the members of our team. They murdered the stuff.*

* Note 7, page 295.

XIX

Coral Sea

In the first week of May, 1942, came a sea fight between a Japanese expeditionary fleet and American
and Australian planes which was probably the decisive
battle of the spring in the Pacific: the so-called Battle
of the Coral Sea. It was certainly Japan's first important
defeat.

The Battle of Midway, a month later, was larger in
conception, bloodier for both sides, and more dis-
astrous to the enemy in material losses; but there was
nothing in it which was not foreshadowed in the Coral
Sea. There, for the first time, the Pacific Allies showed
what they could do by teaming land and sea forces and
equipping them with sound, intelligent foreknowledge
of the enemy's plans and dispositions. There, for the
first time, Japanese seapower was riddled and turned
back by Allied planes. If the Japs did not draw an
object lesson from the Coral Sea in time to avoid exactly similar errors at Midway Island, it was because
their Midway operation was already "on the stove"—

fully planned and reaching the point of execution—at the time of the battle off New Guinea.

It seems to me that the Japanese mistakes and miscalculations of that period deserve to be stressed; certainly they deserved underlining at the time they occurred. Optimism about the Pacific war, half-cocked strutting and muscle-flexing on our part, were and are as dangerous as can be. Perhaps overemphasis of the enemy's power and genius should be the rule. But I doubt it. There are dangers that way, too. If you think back, you'll remember a time—spanning the weeks from the fall of Singapore to the fall of Bataan and the launching of the Japs' Coral Sea armada—when the spectacular successes of the Japanese induced a limp morbidity, a semiparalysis, in certain Allied quarters. Some of us were under a spell, and by no means a healthy one.

The same thing happened when Germany moved from one dumbfounding victory to another in 1939 and 1940. Even after the RAF splintered the Luftwaffe over Britain, we needed cool and eloquent interpreters to persuade us that the Germans were human, militarily, and could blunder—could blunder in conceptions of air strategy, a field in which they were thought to be practically sorcerous.

If the Germans mishandled the new air weapon because of a rooted loyalty to the old army game, the Japs made the same mistake in deference to the old navy game. Their war tradition was fully as much naval as ours or Britain's. If the lesson they "taught" at Pearl Harbor did not keep them from sending forth ships to be wrecked by planes in the Coral Sea and at Midway—well, it is plain that the Allies had no patent on military *faux pas*. Those shoes of Tojo's contain their share of clay.

And this, I think, is a good thing for the people of America and Australia and England to know. The stubbornness of Australians, Americans in Australia, and the Australian government in refusing to believe that there could have been a victory in the Coral Sea—and they were stubborn, believe me—is the measure of their early conviction that the Japs were somehow walking hand in hand with the god of war. I doubt if any alliance can fight its best under such conditions.

Australian spokesmen took their cue from military headquarters and talked for publication of a "possible enemy reverse," but it was clear from their moody rhetoric that they thought they were whistling the old Singapore graveyard tune again at the request of the same old bandmasters, Americans in Australia—army officers, for instance, and war correspondents—were hardly less slow to shake off the effects of five months of bitter reverses sugarcoated by happy communiqués. That is the hell of it. A happy communiqué cloaking defeat sounds just the same to the untrained ear as a happy communiqué announcing a victory. Since the entire history of the major crises of this war has been written, up till now, in communiqués more or less cloudy in tone, we are just beginning to learn the knack of hearing the truth between the lines—just starting to develop an ear for this occult music. It is a silly trick to have to master, and I hope it will soon become obsolete.

Last spring we were still tone deaf to the hidden clues in the happy communiqué. We were pretty suspicious, to boot, and perhaps with reason. Talking with General MacArthur a day or two after the end of the Coral Sea battle, one of my road companions from New Guinea mentioned the battle of Macassar Straits as a possible parallel to the new development. You'll remember the Macassar Straits—running between Borneo and Celebes toward the ill-fated island of Java. MacArthur seemed puzzled by the reference.

"Macassar?" he said politely, arching his eyebrows.

"Well," floundered Knickerbocker, "wasn't it more or less the same process? A Japanese invasion fleet steaming toward an objective, and our planes bombing and torpedoing their ships?"

MacArthur threw back his head and laughed.

"There is a slight difference between Macassar and the Coral Sea," said the general, spreading out his fingers on his desk. "One was a defeat, and the other was a victory."

In the light of subsequent news—and after the last faint fear of a joker in the deck was removed from the last doubting mind—the distinction between Macassar and the Coral Sea, as MacArthur himself explained it, was evident to the world. Jap ships were sunk in the Indies straits, but the Japs moved right ahead to conquest. Jap ships, troop transports as well as warships, were sunk in the Coral Sea—and the Japs turned tail.

The battle which produced this change in the current of Pacific war, or which, at any rate, checked the flow of the first current, was preceded by certain signs and portents. Our forces knew what was coming. I didn't. The Japs made a fan-shaped aerial sortie on April 30-May 1 which practically dogged my footsteps. Within forty-eight hours Japanese planes and I covered 1,200 miles and came to three of the same widely separated places at the same time. Two of these places had never been visited by the enemy before. If I'd been Jack Johnson, former heavyweight champion of the world, I would have known they were following me. Mr. Johnson tells in his autobiography how he was driving in London one night in 1914 when a German zeppelin came overhead, spotted him, and began to hound him through the streets, zigzagging right and left to follow his every move.

"They wanted me bad," says Mr. Johnson.

Since Mr. Johnson was nowhere in our neighborhood this time, I did not know what was indicated by the sudden Japanese interest in Horn Island, tiny Allied air base off the very northernmost point of Australia, and in Townsville, the flat, hot little coastal settlement in northern Queensland, sheltered from the Coral Sea by Australia's Great Barrier Reef. The Coral Sea, three days before the battle, was calm and green as I flew above it in Hatch's bomber. Its waves, from 12,000 feet, looked like tiny wrinkles, and you could barely see where they lapped white about the atolls.

This was the same sea we had sailed in the *Floating Firecracker*. The Barrier Reef hooks up and around Cape York, Australia's equatorial pole, walling off the wild jungle of the cape, and the little islands at its tip, from the east. Aboriginals were the only inhabitants of this region till the building of the Allied airdrome on Horn Island.

There, while we refueled on the ground and ate tea and bread and marmalade and talked baseball, Jap bombers paid their first call of the war, escorted by Zeros. We got away unscathed, wondering if the visit was purely in our honor or whether it had another motivation. When Jap naval guns thundered in the Coral Sea a few days later, it was obvious that the enemy had tried to reconnoiter our bases and positions as thoroughly as he could without giving his show away.

The same errand brought Photo Joe over Townsville the next day, soon after I got there. He had never come so far south before, even with observation planes. After a quick look at the Queensland base, from a point so high above the town that he was out of range of anti-aircraft guns and almost invisible, he went loping hastily home again. His survey of Townsville completed his sweep—a rather gingerly sweep, to be truthful—of the Allied bases he thought he had to reckon with in his next move. When the Japs came south again, they came with ships.

In Townsville that afternoon I heard of the death the day before of Brigadier General Harold H. George, Bataan air chief who had come to Australia with Mac-Arthur, and of Melville Jacoby, young correspondent for *Time* and *Life*. They were killed together in a tragically pointless accident at one of our airfields, when a runaway P-40 cut them down as they climbed out of a bomber that had just landed. From Jacoby and the general the talk at the big hotel on the waterfront swung to the possibilities of invasion of Australia. I found a feeling of trouble in the wind. Townsville had added up the portents of the last day or two and found the sum to be imminent danger from the north. This, remember, was a nervous season in the Australian commonwealth; not so much among the rank and file of people at home, who moved about their business as nonchalantly as Kansans or Missourians, as among the spokesmen, reporters, and paid observers of the war, men infected in varying degree by the loud and frank alarums of the Curtin government. The government quite candidly considered that help in men and material from America at that date was inadequate. It treated with open hostility any talk of second fronts in Europe and all strategies which tended to minimize or bypass the peril to Australia.

There were rumors of Jap ship concentrations behind the mask of islands to the north, New Guinea, New Britain, and the Solomons. These, in fact, were more than rumors. On flights like the one I'd just taken with Hatch and his crew, in bombers and pursuits and observation planes, our flyers had spotted Jap warships, including carriers, where none had been seen a week before.

If this was known to some of us, much more was known to the Army and Navy commands at Melbourne and Pearl Harbor. In the Coral Sea, for the first time.in the war, our forces carried the advantages of surprise and foreknowledge into battle with them. It made a mighty difference. And there were many in Australia, and I suppose at home, who shared the astonishment of the Japanese when an Allied fleet, as well as Allied land planes, came up to confront the southbound enemy.

As you know, this was no naval battle in the traditional sense of the term. The rival fleets never came within shell-range of each other. When the Jap's shock units, his interference, were sighted as they rounded the eastern tip of Papua into the Coral Sea, our heavy and medium land-based bomber planes from island bases and from the Australian mainland poured it on them. Dive bombers followed, and carrier-based jobs, including torpedo planes, and when the Allies picked up the main body of the Jap fleet there were five hundred land and naval planes on hand to chew it to pieces.

On the mainland we saw bomber crews coming home from the battle. Through the red pattern of their tales of square hits on cruisers, carriers, and supply ships, and of Jap planes falling, you could sense the awe and excitement they felt at the sight of their first great sea engagement. If it's true that the airplane in this war is the hound of fate on the warship's traces, it's also true that the warship is still the highest adventure in the flyer's life.

"I've never had a feeling like that," said a bomber pilot just in from his run at the Japanese armada. "There was nothing but ocean down there, as wide as the world. Then way ahead there were suddenly four white flecks, and then I could see them—ships in line. They made four curves, far down below us, and their wakes were wider than the ships were as they turned to get away from us. I had a feeling that everything would go right, that we would score on them, but at the same time everything I did was like a dream. I think it's the bigness and emptiness all around that gets you. You are all alone in the world with those ships on the sea below."

There was reason to believe, from the first-hand, first-flush stories we heard, that the teamwork of our land, sea, and air commands was still not all it might have been in this battle. There were land-based bombers which did not know the whereabouts of our own sea forces; naval men who did not know that land bombers were in the fight. Matters seemed to have improved in this respect when we struck off Midway a month later. The Coral Sea was the first coordinated experiment of its kind, for us, and it was rough around the edges. But it worked.

We lost men and we lost planes and we lost some ships. The gallant carrier *Lexington* had to be abandoned and sunk as she limped home to Hawaii, scarred and smoking. The Japs, in retreat, laid their standard claim to sinking everything American but Hiawatha's canoe. At first, with the memory of the Java Sea fight and Pearl Harbor fresh in our minds, we were tempted to believe them. There was nothing particularly surprising in Australia's hesitation to accept the pleasant truth when it became known, certainly nothing in it so comical as the acrobatics of America's newspaper experts on war.

There was one expert who said, in his first interpretation of the Coral Sea battle: "This is a defeat." The next day he said "This is a victory." The next day, as I understand it, he disappeared from view—the latter action being highly uncharacteristic, to my way of thinking, for the strongest trait of the members of this guild is nonchalance about yesterday's miscues. The military expert is perpetually lighting a Murad, with a cool, insouciant smile, and blocking out his next manifesto with redoubled confidence. I know of a radio prophet and strategist, unmatched today for the stateliness of his views, who pronounced, over a cup of tea in Paris in August, 1939: "My good fellow, there will be no war." He has never taken a backward step since.

It is something else again, I guess, to err on the side of pessimism. That seems to be the unforgivable sin, the misstep which leads the rest of the boys in the experts' fraternity to steal quietly from their fallen comrade's side, leaving him alone with a gun on the table before him.

Australia's reaction to the Coral Sea fight, her official reaction, was what could be expected from past per-

formance. I've said that the government was anxious
at all times to underline the country's peril. When
Richard G. Casey, Australian Minister to the United
States, suddenly left his post to take an appointment
from Winston Churchill as Britain's war minister in
the Middle East, John Curtin was obviously angry—
and not simply because of "interference" or fractures
of diplomatic procedure. The switch of Casey seemed
to him to belittle Australia's own interests and play up
another zone of war at Australia's expense.

His attitude was not so selfish as it may have seemed
ten thousand miles away. If enemy ships, planes, and
guns lay based in the West Indies; if Havana were
under threat by land and sea; if Key West and New
Orleans had been systematically bombed—well, the
situation in the United States would match the situation of Australia as Curtin conceived it to be in the
first months of Pacific war. The government and the
press had no sympathy whatever for second fronts in
Europe, and they were plainly allergic to reports of
American troop movements to Ireland and England.
Their feeling illustrated one of the first and funda-
mental problems of the United Nations' alliance. It
presented our central board of strategy with one of
the toughest nuts it had—or has—to crack.

After Australia accepted the Coral Sea battle, warily,
as a success, the newspapers proceeded to take it for

granted, along with the government, that Japan's objective here had been invasion of Australia. This view was somewhat at variance with the opinion of General MacArthur's command, which believed at the time and later announced, from what it knew of the form and nature of the Jap expedition, that Port Moresby was the immediate target. Moresby, bypassed, would become an active counter-threat to any Japanese move on Australia.

"You can't outflank an air base as you would a land base," I was told by one of MacArthur's ranking strategists. "If the air base is 'cut off' instead of wiped out, it remains in action, and forms a danger to the flanker."

Be that as it may (and the Jap's preoccupation with Moresby, before and since, seems to bear out the Mac-Arthur view), the Curtin government was inclined to regard the argument as a quibble. It did not alter the basic position. If Australia was not saved, there and then, by the Battle of the Coral Sea, she was saved indirectly—or the government and the press did not know salvation when they saw it.

XX

Diggers at Work

THERE was no doubt about the disposition in Canberra, seat of the Australian federal government, to rate the Yank's assistance highly, celebrate his arrival in the Southwest Pacific, and make him feel like quite a man. The press also slapped him on the back at every suitable opportunity. There was some danger, I suppose, of the American soldier's head becoming too wide for his hatband, if he read the newspapers and listened to the local radio.

This peril was punctured at birth, however, by the stout resistance of the Australian people to anything supine or mawkish in the way of gratitude. And the Digger, the soldier of the species, went even further in his determination to keep the Yank's feet on the ground. After all, why should he baby his ally from overseas when he did not permit his own officers too many liberties?

The Digger does not call generals by their first names, but he likes to make it clear that he might, if so disposed. Each Australian is his own government,

224

to a large extent, in private life, and he changes very little when they put a uniform on his back. The Digger is a tough character. He is kindly, hospitable, and gay, but tough. Army life does not destroy his individuality, to put it mildly, nor does it blind him to the practical aspects of life. The story has come back from Libyan fronts, too often to be wholly fictional, of the Aussie who yelled to a comrade, as they charged a machine-gun nest, "If the food in this bloody outfit don't get better soon, Alf, I'm going home!"

The faceless men of the German and Japanese armies are beyond the comprehension of the Digger. If he fails to understand them, however, he resents them and what they imply from the very pit of his belly.

Does his independence, which is as hard to pin and crush as a cat's, make for ragged discipline in the field of battle? That has been said. I have even heard examples cited. It's probably true that the Digger works best on jobs of individual fighting. He is a good rifleman and machine-gunner, a great flyer, and more often than not, a wholehearted fighter with a bayonet. When the Aussies laid ambush to Japanese attempting to land at Milne Bay, at the eastern tip of New Guinea, they held high harvest with their bayonets, slogging forward through mud calf-deep to bring the fight home to the enemy with steel. The ease of their victory led some of them, veterans from Africa, to belittle the

Jap and rate him below the German as a soldier. This, of course, was just as reckless as the judgment which says that no Australian can take discipline. Farther west in Papua, in the mountains around Port Moresby, the Digger found the Jap fighting a fight of his own making, under his own conditions, and collected pretty good evidence of the yellow man's skill at sniping, his fanatic courage, his shrewdness, and his durability.

Even there, though, the Digger was surprisingly quick to adapt himself to circumstances—circumstances by no means appetizing to the soldier with a so-called "realistic" attitude toward war. There's a difference, perhaps, beween the realism of the Digger and the realism of the Italian soldier. For one thing, the Digger feels he is fighting his own war. For another, he likes to fight.

He is strong, sentimental, stubborn, variable, sly, frank, and acquisitive. A magazine correspondent in Australia, a good fellow but inclined to measure all forms of humanity by the standards of the easy-to-pigeonhole Teutons, among whom he had spent much time, complained to me that the Digger was peculiar and not completely noble.

"If these fellows are so damn rugged, independent, and all the rest of it," he said, "why do they stand around the dock, when an American troopship comes

in, scrambling for coins that our men throw them?
Is that independent?"

It is a very independent operation, as the Digger
performs it. He hears that the Yank is apt to make the
gesture described above. What the Yank's motive may
be, apart from the fact that he is rich and overpaid and
in some cases chuckleheaded enough to perform the
extravaganza of throwing away money, is no concern
of the Digger's. The Digger likes to acquire money,
or any other tangible form of property. There is no
false shame about him. On the other hand, no man in
the world is more devoid of servility. If you suggested
he was begging, he would punch you in the nose. He
would do likewise if you impugned his honor or his
patriotism. I saw a Digger stiffen a very large American
sailor in a taproom one evening, for a long series of
reasons, the last and decisive one being that the sailor
said the doorknobs in the city of Adelaide were set too
low in the doors. They were a little low, at that, but the
Digger came staunchly to their defense.

"That's all bloody right about our —— doorknobs,"
he said, just prior to throwing his right.*

That led to one of the few free-for-alls I saw between
Yanks and Australians. For the main part, the Digger
extended to our soldiers a cordiality fuller and freer
than most of them had ever seen at home. He admired

* Note 8, page 297.

their startling efficiency at engineering, construction, and organization jobs, marveled at the high quality of their uniforms and food and equipment, held his own or better in the field of kidding and repartee, and in general had no fault to find with the Yanks except that they were too polite to live—at any rate, too bloody polite.

Many a Digger from the country Outback was at roughly the same stage of evolution in the social graces that Charles Dickens confronted when he saw America just one hundred years ago. Dickens took refuge in his cambric handkerchief, being a quick man with a cambric handkerchief. The Yanks, not far removed from first principles themselves, saw nothing especially outlandish in the behavior of the Digger, and they were puzzled to find themselves regarded by a good many Australian girls as models of Chesterfieldian elegance, just because they rose in their seats when a lady joined or left them. It was the Dodsworth formula with reverse English.

I heard Diggers grumble about the sickening overuse of "Thank you" and "Please" by Yanks. I also heard them cavil at the inefficiency of Yank table manners, and here they had something. Americans certainly are too stylized and roundabout in the way they handle their weapons at mealtime, especially in the shifting of the fork from the left to the right hand after cutting meat. This struck the Australians, and with reason, as impractical.

The Digger put the Yank to shame in several of the finer arts as well, among them the singing of songs. Americans in recent years have grown noticeably self-conscious and lackadaisical about group singing. There is no such curse on the free souls of the Australians. Like the Russians, they break into fine and spontaneous song wherever they gather. They are at home throughout the speckled range of American popular music, from *Old Black Joe* through *You Wore a Tulip* down to *Chattanooga Choochoo*. They have scores of songs from their ancestral homelands, England, Ireland, and Scotland. And they have their own songs—folk-slang, as in *Waltzing Matilda;* the Army and Tin Pan Alley wedded, British style, as in *Bless 'Em All;* and good vigorous come-all-ye's in the modern Australian idiom, which is singleminded but straight to the point, as in:

> "Fellehs of Us-trilieh,
>   Blokes and coves and coots,
>   Shift yer bloody carcasses,
>   Move yer bloody boots.
>   Gird yer bloody loins up,
>   Get yer bloody gun,
>   Set the bloody enemy
>   And watch the bugger run.

Chorus: Get a bloody move on,
            Have some bloody sense;
            Learn the bloody art of
            Self-de-bloody-fense.

            Fellehs of Us-trilieh,
            Cobbers, chaps, and mites,
            Hear the bloody enemy
            Kickin' at the gites.
            Blow the bloody bugle,
            Beat the bloody drum,
            Upper-cut and out the cow
            To Kingdom-bloody-Come!"

The term "cow" approximates heel, louse, or bum in American, and is called on to do a good deal of approximating. It's hard to predict just what words, if any, the Yanks will take home with them out of Australia's rich body of slang. Given sufficiently long exposure to the Digger's language, which is not all "bloody" and Anglo-Saxon participles, though it sounds that way at first, we might well adopt a phrase here and there, for the pickings are good.

When I left Australia, Americans were still holding fast to "swell" and "lousy," while the Australians remained true to "beaut" and "crook," which mean the same things respectively. But there were signs of a possible interchange of culture.

"For example," said an Australian captain, "my men are using 'goddam' quite a lot more than they did before you chaps came here. Very interesting expression."

The Yanks, on the other hand, had become infected at least to the point of saying "Cheers!" whenever they hoisted a drink. One American Army doctor, learning that Australia had a slang word for "this afternoon," to wit, "sarvo," brought it into his conversation at the slightest provocation—which can be, and was, a little annoying.

It was pleasant to find that rhyming slang, of which I had heard a great deal from world travelers in the boxing and wrestling rackets, was by no means dead in Australia. The Diggers referred to money as "oscar," to feet as "plates," to a wife as "trouble," to a blue mood or hangover as "the joes." All these terms have their roots deep in an ancient singsong jargon that grew up in England and Scotland, among carnival hustlers and purse-snatchers and gentlemen who lived by their wits, more than two centuries ago.

Like pig Latin and a dozen other simple codes, rhyming slang was designed to baffle cops, bailiffs, suckers, inquisitive customers, interlopers—anybody who might be "on the Erie," as the American jail phrase goes; in short, listeners-in. It was no such intricate cipher as Edgar Allan Poe would have built for thieves and conspirators—just a jingle, one step removed from the fact. Instead of calling, "I'll meet you at York" to his mate as he broke for cover, the pickpocket yelled "Mutton and pork!" In time, like most outlaw slang, this became the innocent property of the ordinary citizen, and in time too, naturally enough, its phrases were beheaded and curtailed and streamlined by constant use, till the original roots were lost from sight.

The London householder, describing his Saturday afternoon to chums at the pub, might say:

"Then I took the trouble and the godfers for a whisper in the fields before rosie."

What he did was take his wife and children for a walk in the street before tea—which follows, as night follows day, from the fact that "trouble and strife" means wife, that "God Forbids" are kids, that "whisper and talk" is walk, that "fields of wheat" mean street, and that tea is represented lyrically by "Rosie Lee."

Australia in her early days was settled and peopled by so many restless spirits and men of the highway with a mastery of this jargon that it came to be known in some quarters, as time went on, as Australian slang. When the Digger says "oscar," he is harking back to Oscar Ash, or cash. "Plates," for feet, stems from plates of meat. The "joes" are the Joe Blakes, meaning shakes.

There is more Australian slang in the appendix of this book. Meanwhile, the student of life in all its phases cannot afford to ignore another field of culture, a second meeting-ground of Yank and Digger. To put it baldly, Americans and Australians are two of the gamblingest peoples on the face of the earth. And wartime Australia, like wartime America, provides ample facilities for the exercise of this pastime.

The nearest that Yanks at home could come to legitimate number-playing was the Irish Sweepstakes, which died a few years ago and was only quasi-legal at best in America. Australia has public state lotteries here and there, like the Golden Casket in Queensland and Tat's (for Tattersall's) in Tasmania. Her horse-racing, as I said before, is confined to Saturdays as a wartime measure, but on that day the operator who knows his way around—the Digger, for instance, who seems to know the history, background, and habits of every thoroughbred in the country—can bet on ten to twenty races at each of half a dozen tracks simultaneously. At a Sydney track I wandered into a ring of bookmakers shouting odds on horses whose names did not jibe at all with the names on my program. It was a ring complete in itself and autonomous, with its own slates, parasols, and checkered weskits—and it did business on nothing but the races at Melbourne, six hundred miles away. It was a Digger from Perth who tipped me off.

"If you want to bet those Melbourne races, Yank, just sigh so," he said, "and I'll give you some good ones."

"You know the horses down there?"

"Like my own brothers," said the Digger serenely.

The fact is, though, that gambling is a simple, home-spun pursuit that needs no help from public paraphernalia like totalizators, bookmaking rings, and lotteries to thrive. If there are fewer crap games in American camps abroad than at home, it's because we have fewer soldiers abroad, as yet. Redistribution of the month's payload, over a pair of dice, is still standard procedure in the Army, and will doubtless remain so as long as war exists, to the painful confusion of mothers and other reactionaries.

Any brace of numbered bones will start a dice game anywhere, and any pair of coins will start a game of Two-Up among Diggers. The men of the two armies have yet to mingle thoroughly, and they continue frozen to some extent in their respective cultures—which is to say that the Yanks cling to dice and the Australians to Two-Up. In time, the association may produce that broad, flexible interchange of ideas on which modern civilization is based. It took the Yank no time at all to learn that a "place" bet on a horse in Australia is good for third place as well as second.

Being anxious to study every aspect of Anzac life,

I made a considerable survey of the ritual of Two-Up. It cost me about nine florins, or eighteen shillings, and was just about worth it; certainly not a dime more. There is hardly any difference between Two-Up and the American luncheon and barroom practice of matching coins. One player tosses his coin first, and the other, inspecting the fall, tries to guess before tossing his own whether the result will be odd or even. The two coins themselves are usually the stake. The players alternate in tossing first. For some reason or other, Australians infallibly divine which side of a coin tossed by a Yank will come up. In this game, therefore, the Yank is what would be known in rhyming slang as Mr. Tucker; i.e., sucker.

Two-Up is as universal a practice in Australia as shaving or bathing. No Yank, however, should let himself be coaxed into playing it on the street or up an alleyway. The cops, or Johns, move in on public Two-Up games, just as they often do on open-air dice forums at home.

I don't want to give the impression that dice, the recreation of the Emperor Augustus, is absolutely unknown in Australia. The country has, or did have, its gambling houses, and therefore its house games, dice among them—a variation of house craps as practiced in Palm Beach, Saratoga, Kansas City, and other temples of the trade. Perhaps it's significant that I saw my first Australian dice layout in the boisterous and hell-bent little port of Darwin, where anything and every-thing went before Jap bombs emptied the town. An Australian officer, Lieutenant Bass, ran a little single-sheet army newspaper there, printed on a flatbed press in a shack across the road from the shrapnel-shattered general hospital. Here he had gathered souvenirs of Darwin's rowdy days before the bombs came, including the cloth layout of the dice game called "Ins and Outs." The customer bet even money on whether the dice would come even or odd—"in" or "out." He could also pick a point on any roll and take the conventional odds —thirty to one for snake-eyes or any other double, ten to one for any ten or four, etc.

Lieutenant Bass became an outstanding hero in Darwin in the pre-Jap days, thanks to blind luck and the passion of the Digger garrison for racing. He printed racing selections, as a circulation-builder, and being the paper's entire staff and only available handi-capper, he picked the winners himself—out of a hat, since he did not know one horse from another. On his first try he had seven winners at one track.

"My fame from then on was absolutely sensational," said Bass modestly. "The chaps used to flock about the office and grab for papers as they came off the press."

The Digger in quest of anything, from a fortune at the races to a bottle of beer, is as single-hearted and intent as a bird dog. Two Diggers retreating hell-for-leather from Crete, in the wake of their company, paused long enough to salvage a typewriter from a burning house, while the Luftwaffe raked the ground around them. They added it to the pack they were lugging and carried it for hundreds of miles, in shifts, against the day they would find time to sit down and write their letters home—in proper style this time, and none of your bloody scrawls. The day came, and they opened the typewriter: to find that the letters on the keyboard were Greek! Their language on this occasion, according to one of their officers, lowered all previous records.

Since the Australian soldier is never the slave of convention, it did not surprise bystanders and bathers around the swimming compound at Port Moresby greatly when a pair of Diggers arrived one morning to fish for their noonday meal with a hand grenade and a couple of sticks of the high explosive known as gelignite. We simply got out of the way as fast as possible.

The compound was a rectangle of harbor water fenced off from sharks. The fishing was only fair. The two Izaak Waltons surveyed the situation and studied their tackle. They elected to open proceedings with the grenade. At the first cast, a couple of small mackerel came reluctantly to the surface, and were scooped in.

The Diggers didn't get a bite with the gelignite. All they got was a piece of the bottom of the sea, which also came up reluctantly.

Experts on the sidelines concluded that gelignite is no good for mackerel, though it might work with salmon or brook trout.

I suppose the Australian army, regulars and militiamen alike, comes close to being the sort of people's army that Lord Strabolgi and other critics of the military status quo in England have clamored for. Most of its officers rise from the ranks. Others come direct from their jobs and homesteads, as Cincinnatus came from the plow. University professors are camouflage experts. Young men in the service invent or develop equipment that the Army now uses, such as submachine guns, and carry right on with their duties. The desert general, Sir Iven Mackay, is a school teacher who calls soldiering his "recreation" in *Who's Who*. The commander-in-chief in Australia, General Sir Thomas Blamey, was a police chief.

No officer with a touch of "wowser" in him—Australian for stuffed shirt—will get far with Digger troops. The Digger is a newcomer among the world's democrats and still vigilant in defense of his birthright, in war or in peace. Submersion is not for him. If the Yanks feel the same way, they at least show an overlayer of complaisance, of willingness to suspend self-expression for the moment, that comes perhaps of a century and a half of independence and the secure knowledge of independence. The Digger is closer than the Yank to the soldier of Washington's army who felt there was unfinished business on his flanks as well as a foe before him.

The Australian soldier is the best among the Allies by athletic standards—well-developed muscles, quick reflexes, and sharp eyes. The American Army, which looks next best by this yardstick, can show as many men who are fit, say, to fight in a prize-ring, but they come from a population of 130,000,000. There are 7,000,000 Australian people in all, and they seldom produce a soldier whom you would care to meet in a back room with fists, knives, pistols, or teeth.

I am giving his opponent the best of it, too, when I specify teeth, for that is the only weakness the well-kept American is apt to detect in the Australian soldier. It's not a weakness that keeps him out of action—more than one otherwise lethal Digger simply has his bad teeth yanked summarily and replaced by synthetic fangs, a uniform, and a bayonet. The eyes of the Australians are much better than ours, in general. One of the things that strikes them about us is the number of Yanks wearing spectacles.

Big-boned and clear-eyed, one Aussie soldier looks a good deal like another, even to the cast of his features—for the Australians are of undiluted British or Irish stock and have all been molded together in the single task of scratching a subsistence and a civilization from a continent that is worn and bare and unyielding. They have lived a life that cultivates sinews in the body and a fierce self-sufficiency in the mind.

On the Yank who thinks of patronizing them, they have the same effect as a pitcher of icewater, applied externally.

XXI

Behind the Lines

CAMPED near Melbourne was one of the first American Army divisions to reach Australia. It was a rarity at the time I saw it, in the spring of 1942 (middle autumn down yonder), and worth a visit just for a look at "honest" troops, as they were called by officers with nostalgic roots in the last war.

This has been a hard war to get used to, for the old-line soldier. The first year's fighting in the Pacific was done by airmen, sailors, Marines, coast artillery (anti-aircraft), and amphibious specialists of whom certain types did not even exist in 1917. In the war zone, these were all the correspondent saw. Only the Philippine garrison sent infantry into action, outnumbered, ill-equipped, and by no means representative of the carefully barbered "military might" that the First World War taught us to think in terms of. The fighting at Darwin, New Guinea, and the Solomons was completely Johnny-come-lately.

There's no doubt in my mind that the high command in Washington still considers this war of air and island to be preliminary, skirmish stuff. To America's European front, where we could plan our campaign and move in an ordered way, we sent divisional troops as an opening move—not actually to "open" the front, but because they seemed to be the logical symbol of good faith and armed assistance.

In the Pacific there was no time for symbols. We were attacked, and so we grabbed for the handiest weapons and fought as urgency directed. This sort of fighting set the pattern for some time to come. It was a pattern that did not jibe entirely with the naval type of war that many strategists, armchair and otherwise, insisted on for the Pacific. Our year of island war has made it a commonplace that beachheads are needed for land attack and that beachheads are won by relatively small shock forces protected and powered by air.

Just the same, each army division set ashore in Ireland was resented by Australia and each division sent to Australia was richly welcomed and lovingly taken stock of—even though such divisions could be counted comfortably at first on the fingers of the right hand of a celebrated Chicago pitcher, Mr. Mordecai "Three-Fingered" Brown.

It's true that the immediate plans of MacArthur and the Pacific naval leaders called for no large force of land troops; more accurately, I believe the immediate plans of Washington called for no such force. But Australia had a different view of the war. To understand Australia's feeling about reinforcement or lack of reinforcement, you have constantly to keep in mind the fact that Australia expected, made herself expect, invasion. This was a condition that prevailed well into the middle of 1942, and naturally it colored the country's attitude toward the scattered land troops that were sent her way.

The Yankee leaders themselves could not afford to ignore the possibility of invasion, last spring. Visiting the X Division in the pale green hills north of Melbourne, I found its commander driving his men vigorously through their paces.

"The boys are still a little raw," he said—America had only been at war a few months—"but give me four more weeks for this sort of thing and I'll have them ready for what may come."

Standing on a low hilltop, we watched commissioned officers stalk and crawl through maneuvers they in turn would teach the enlisted men next day. An advance scout, a captain, came in view along the crest. He spotted a nest of enemy resistance beyond the next valley and signaled the "troops" behind him. They followed, hugging the curve of the hillside to avoid silhouetting and exposing themselves to enemy fire until the nest could be wiped out.

Now and then a rabbit scuttled from stump to stump

across land for which its owners were paid "a reasonable percentage of the normal yield" for its use as Yank camp ground.

At the time, there was no larger concentration of Yank troops in Australia than this one. Wandering around the camp, playing poker, shooting dice, riding jeeps, listening in, I found that the X Division's camp, like all camps, had its own special quality, its own customs and songs and sayings, its own slang. "Hot stuff coming!" was the common synonym for "Watch out" or "Make way," carried ashore from the ships in convoy, where the waiters at mess, holding their trays aloft, used it to pave a road for hot food en route from the kitchen.

The star of the camp was the chaplain, a music-lover of infinite resource and sagacity, Colonel E. Raymond Attebery. His library of phonograph records was not only the largest and most various to be found in the Southwest Pacific, but the shack in which he housed it was the only perpetual free music clinic I have ever seen.

The chaplain had "begged" and "hustled" his something more than three hundred records before the X Division left America's west coast for Australia—in the army phrase, he "promoted" them. Putting the arm on a department store here and a music company there, he assembled specimens ranging from Jimmy

Lunceford to Beethoven and skipping no stops in between.

"I promoted at least two hundred besides the three hundred we have here, for that matter," he told me, "but left them behind for want of room. Do you know what I left behind? Chiefly classical stuff, to make more room for swing records. And do you know what I find here? The boys like the classics just as well as the rhythm numbers. That is wonderfully encouraging," said Chaplain Attebery wistfully, "and I wish I had brought more classics."

The chaplain was a short, square, bright-eyed man, nuts for music, as the boys said. His firm belief was that soldiers in camp enjoy music more than anything in the world except letters from home; and I have never seen anything to indicate that he was wrong.

The fountainhead of his minstrelsy, an eight-by-ten shack, contained a phonograph hooked up with a public address system that carried the sound of his concerts to every man and beast within a radius of five miles. However, the chaplain had to be doubly sure that no one was overlooked. Any time he felt that the troops in the outskirts of the camp were not deriving the full benefit of his mighty entertainment, he stowed a recording machine aboard a portable sound truck, took down a few dozen selections from his shelves, and drove off to bolster these weak points in his lines.

One way and another, there was music day and night. When I left the concert hall at midnight one evening, the phonograph was still going strong, and the chaplain's assistants on the late shift—a pair of corporals who studied the organ and piano respectively in private life—were still working steadily, one at the controls, the other laying out fresh records and acknowledging requests from outlying sectors over the telephone.

The telephone was the voice of the people, and it represented a tiny dark cloud in the chaplain's life. The chaplain was a classics man. He could stomach rhythm records, having a hearty digestion, but he was tone deaf to boogie-woogie. Along about ten o'clock at night, the soldiers became exclusively swing-hungry, and from then on they requested hotter and hotter records. This was the signal for the chaplain, a tactful and generous man, to scrap his own tastes, shake hands all around, and quietly disappear from the shack, leaving his staff to cater to the appetites of the musically damned.

When I met him, pottering eagerly among the shelves of music that lined his library, he was in an operatico-spiritual mood, but willing to oblige guests.

"Recognize this?" he said, nodding toward the phonograph. "Duet from *Naughty Marietta*, with Jan Peerce and Ann Jamieson."

"Yes," I said. "There's a record of Gershwin's *Looking for a Boy* where Ann Jamieson hits a note, the third above the high tonic, that sort of—"

"I don't doubt it," said the chaplain enthusiastically. "But look, I want you to hear Caruso in *Pagliacci*. It does him justice. And while we're playing that"—he turned to a corporal—"let's see if you can find *Tales from Hoffman* and perhaps line up some Kreisler and Rubinstein, and Harold Bauer playing the *Moonlight Sonata,* and Roland Hayes singing *Were You There?*"

"Somebody just 'phoned in for *Indian Love Call,*" said the corporal.

"All right, find that, too," said Chaplain Attebery tolerantly. "That's nice."

I will not mention what the chaplain had on his shelves in detail, except to say that there were American waltzes, Viennese waltzes, patriotic songs, songs of the last war, Hawaiian songs, spirituals, songs of the synagogue, light opera songs, grand opera songs, Sibelius melodies, folk songs, symphony, chamber music, and jive. There was music by Romberg, Gershwin, Kern, Berlin, and Duke Ellington; by Mozart, Brahms, Debussy, Ravel, Gilbert and Sullivan, Wagner, and Liszt. There were songs sung by Lily Pons, Paul Robeson, John McCormack, Dinah Shore, Gene Austin, Lanny Ross, and Gigli. There was swing by Goodman, Dorsey, Shaw, Bradley, Miller, and Armstrong. There was *Rhapsody in Blue* and *Stardust* and *The Barber of Seville* and the ageless popular tunes like *Avalon* and *Chasing Rainbows* and *Moonlight Bay* and *The World Is Waiting for the Sunrise.*

The telephone rang, with an urgent summons to lay off the corn and placate public opinion with *The Wong Wong Blues,* as conceived by Henry Busse. The chaplain glanced nervously at his watch.

"I wanted this young man to hear Marian Anderson —*Deep River.* Do you think. . . ." He gave the corporal an uneasy look. The corporal winked.

"We'll stand 'em off with *Wong Wong,* then slip in *Deep River,*" he said.

"Everyone will want to hear it really," said the chaplain, cheering up. "It's magnificent. But we should be under the stars when we listen," he added, and drew your correspondent outdoors. There, standing in the middle of a camp street in the darkness, ten thousand miles from home, we heard the strains of the Burleigh spiritual swelling over tents, huts, and shacks, and the rich sweet voice of the singer filling every corner of the little Australian valley. When the song ended, the chaplain shook hands, said good-night and walked home to his quarters.

I noticed the division's commander taking the air in front of his own shack a few doors away. I pointed out that he probably had the most musical encampment in the history of warfare.

"I reckon so," said the general inscrutably.

"You like music?" I asked him. After all, he was living there at the very brink of the mightiest flood of decibels west of San Francisco.

"I can't tell one tune from another," said the general, calmly scratching his ear. "The chaplain says it is very obliging of me to let this go on. And it is. Damned obliging.

From camps like the X Division's, Yank soldiers streamed into the city of Melbourne of a Saturday and Sunday, on leave, and threaded their way through streets already thick with headquarters troops, looking for something to do. Things got better in this respect as the weeks passed—that is, the Yanks could find movies in town on Sunday, after the authorities loosened up the blue laws, and sometimes even a bed to sleep in; though certainly not at the hotels. The hotels were jampacked, chiefly with headquarters men, and the lobbies were alive with generals. In the bar of the Hotel Australia I watched a buck private, seasoned with eight or nine stoups of Scotch, sit down at a table with a couple of major generals and open negotiations with a winning smile.

"I like generals," he said, which should have won the sympathy of his audience from the start. "I want to be a general myself. How do you get this way, boys? What do I hafta do?"

The generals coughed politely, and looked over their guest's shoulder, where disaster in the form of two MP's was rapidly moving down on him.

"But there's one thing I don't like about generals," the private was saying, when he suddenly disappeared with a whisking sound as the law took hold.

I know it is felt now, in Washington and elsewhere, that Melbourne was not the best place for Allied Headquarters: twenty-five hundred miles from the fighting lines. At the start of the Pacific war, however, every move was based on the possibility of the Japanese invading Australia. It was thought to be a live possibility, and Melbourne, divided by the width of the continent from Darwin and Port Moresby, looked like the right spot.

All told, the association of more than a million civilians and thousands of armed troops, both Australian and American, has produced surprisingly little friction. It did produce one crime, or series of crimes, that attracted the city's newspapers, though they handled this, practically their first tabloid story of the war, with firm self-control. Three women in the city were found murdered by strangling within the space of a few days. These killings and the news of them failed to create the tremors and neighborhood panics you read of in the mass-murder stories of Thomas Burke and Mrs. Lowndes. Melbourne took them pretty well in stride, and when an American soldier with a record of degeneracy in civilian life was arrested and swiftly collected by the American Army for trial, conviction, and execution, the sensation died a quiet death.

There was a time soon after the Yanks began arriving when American soldiers showed what might be called a tendency, in a small way, to marry, if not to kill, Australian girls. These marriages aroused no enthusiasm whatever, except among the soldiers and the girls. The first outspoken protest came from a bishop in Queensland, who was joined in his stand by a bishop in New South Wales and then, if I remember correctly, by a bishop in Victoria. The general feeling among the authorities seemed to be that there was a time and a place for everything. The American Army, feeling the same way, began to do some unofficial but firm discouraging of the practice, and pretty soon it dwindled to a point where, by summer of 1942, there were only sporadic reports of nuptials breaking out here and there like scattered, unspent firecrackers on the morning of the fifth of July.

I saw the contracting parties in just one of these marriages. Since it united a lieutenant of the air corps with a society girl, it was by way of being fashionable, and got favorable notices in the papers. Not even a prelate demurred.

The soldier in Melbourne was better off for some of the comforts of life than the civilian—cigarettes, for instance, and clothing. When cloth rationing first set in, the civilian could not stalk a new nightshirt before *10 A.M.* without running the risk of death by trampling or after *10* with any certainty that there was a nightshirt left in town. Most of the tobacco shops were permanently out of cigarettes—Australian cigarettes, which Americans dislike, and American cigarettes, which many Australians dislike. The Yank soldier, however, could go to one of a half dozen post exchanges for wearing apparel and for smokes in copious quantities. It's true that his cigarette allotment was narrowed when American brands began to turn up in the hands of bootleggers and scalpers on the streets, retailing for several shillings a pack.

He was lucky to be in a headquarters city. I saw cigarettes—Piedmonts in special small white boxes, put up by the Army for emergency—that were doled as carefully to men in Darwin in the garrison's early days as swallows of water in an open boat.

On leave in MacArthur's town, then, the Yanks went to the movies or the races or the bars or simply walked the streets; all but the few who were keen enough to scent out a pastime which does as much as the great

Flemington race track and the Melbourne Cup to make the city the sporting capital of Australia—in short, football, Australian rules.

This game is as dear to Melbourne as the Dodgers and baseball to Brooklyn. It takes the place in the State of Victoria of the National and American Leagues and Judge Landis's whole shooting gallery. I know that most Americans in Australia pined unremittingly for baseball and their own kind of football, but I also know that those who discovered Australian football and sought it out on Saturday afternoons found a very substantial substitute.

Even the native fan who "barracks" (roots) most faithfully for one or another of Victoria's good professional teams will tell you not to try to understand every statute and bylaw. The umpires pack a rulebook as fat as a Montgomery Ward catalogue, from which they continually cite chapter, verse, and precedent to the baffled players themselves. I will say in justice to the players, though, that they do not listen much. They have neither the time nor the inclination to do so. The game is fast and rough, more like hockey or basketball than American football in its steady action and position play. It actually deserves the name of football more than our game, thanks to the outright genius of the Australian player with his feet. He can hit sixpence from forty yards away with a kick and leave thruppence change.

It does the Yank's heart good, though it may make him homesick, to perceive that the Australian crowd tolerates no nonsense from the umpire. As soon as I heard a yell of "Wike up, melonhead!" from a youth aged ten standing beside me—a large part of the spectators stand—and realized that this courteous petition was aimed at the arbitrator, I knew that all was well with Australian football.

Prowling through the dressing-rooms before a game one Saturday, watching Bluey Truscott's reception by his teammates, inhaling the old familiar clubhouse smells of liniment and tape and sweat, I met a soldier on a motorman's holiday. He was a stocky lieutenant from Los Angeles, with a soft voice and a broken nose, Lieutenant Norman D. Duncan. Six days a week he worked as sports administrator for all the American forces in Australia. On the seventh, his day off, he came like me to hang around the nearest big ball game and talk with the players. We even ate hot dogs, for old time's sake; the Australian hot dog is by no means contemptible, though it cannot match the *chien chaud* as fashioned, say, by Anatole, chef at Yankee Stadium, or César, *maître de cuisine* at Ebbets Field.

Duncan's life would have been miserable without a clubhouse to haunt and athletes to mix with, after years of college football (at the University of California at Los Angeles), pro football, boxing, scouting, and coaching. His own office was always full of athletes, blending business with the pleasures of reminiscence. I found little Tod Morgan there one day. Morgan, born Bert Pilkington in Sequim, Washington, U. S. A., was a good lightweight fighter who wandered off to Australia one time in 1933, looked around, and never went home again. Now, at the age of forty, he was still fighting occasionally—and like Duncan, promoting sports for soldiers.

"Tod just brought me this glove," said Duncan, holding up a gymnasium boxing glove, big as a pillow. "This is the baby I've been looking for: fourteen ounces. That's what the boys will use, twelves and fourteens. They'll produce knockdowns, see, but they won't cut a kid up."

America, after planting quantities of land troops in Australia with no immediate war to fight, neglected to send them any equipment for games, the thing they needed most. Duncan started with his program in his hat and brought Australian equipment—footballs, baseballs, bats, gloves, wrestling mats, boxing rings, volleyballs. He scheduled touch football rather than contact football for the troops, but he had a private dream: to stage a real game before crowds in Sydney or Mel-

bourne on the Fourth of July—wintertime in Australia—between two teams of college and professional
players drawn from the American Army. Long beforehand he sent home a request for sixty football outfits.
They did not come, and the game was not played in
1942. It may be, before the war is over; on July 4, if
Duncan has his way.

I've yet to see the general or admiral in a war zone
who shared the view of some at home that games are
of no importance to soldiers or impair their efficiency.
The Germans have a fairly efficient land army, and
they seem to attach importance to this war; yet any
time a German athlete breaks a world's record for hopping 3 miles and eight-nineteenths, the news is bla-
zoned forth. If Germany still had the heavyweight
boxing champion (as she might, but for the grace of
Providence and Sergeant Joe Louis), we would never
hear the end of it.

One Australian outfit, quartered Outback, used
Bren gun carriers to clear a field of play, and five hundred of its seven hundred men participated in football
games the day the work was finished. I've spoken of the
lone football the South Dakotans used to toss around
in the jungle when they were stationed at Darwin—
and you may have heard that the Marines at Guadal-
canal, within a week of the time they gained their first

foothold on that bloody battleground, with enemy fire still crackling in their ears and bombs falling around them, set up a blackboard beneath the palms and posted the baseball scores in the National League pennant race where all could see.

I spent my final days in Australia in Melbourne. It was the Yankee capital there, the city seen and settled by more Yanks than any other in the country. It is a fine, leafy town, with broad streets and green parks and rows of quiet, comfortable homes. The soldier sent abroad to fight can do worse than wait his turn in the Melbourne region.

A day or two before I left, Joe Dearing, plump photographer, came up with a stack of fresh prints in his hand.

"Is there any argument about the Yanks doing all right down here?" he said.

"All right?"

"With the girls?"

"Not that I know of, Joe."

"I got this one at night, in the park, with a flash," said Dearing. "It's not posed, mind you. I just happened to catch 'em this way. I thought it was sort of symbolic."

At one end of the park bench in the photograph sat an American soldier and a girl, in a clinch. At the other end of the bench sat a Digger, with his chin in his hand, staring bleakly off through the trees. I don't know if Joe ever turned the picture in for publication. It was, as he said, sort of symbolic—of the fact that Australia is a nice place to go when you travel, if nothing else.

XXII

The Tasman Bumps

We were three days in New Zealand. According to the bylaws of the unofficial guild of World Travelers with Typewriters, with which is combined the informal fraternity of Deep Thinkers at a Moment's Notice, you cannot write a definitive work on the life, customs, character, and significance of a country without spending a minimum of five days there. As we go to press there is legislation pending to reduce this term of required study to ninety hours flat, but I don't think it will get anywhere. Control is still in the hands of the Tories.

And that is just as well, considering that our stay in the port of Wellington, which is all we saw of New Zealand, was a blur of lashing rain and wild wind and no cabs and no place to sleep. To be truthful, they did have a few spare beds in the city, but Raymond and I, whenever three o'clock in the morning came around, found that these had all been shuffled and dealt and claimstaked.

So we would buck our way down the waterfront

street toward the docks, leaning into the wind, and fetch up in our bunks aboard the ship that had brought us there, to spend what was left of the night. Shipboard seemed the right place to be, at that, in the sort of gale that blew through Wellington.

You approach New Zealand from Australia by a sea route that is known—or might well be known—as the Tasman Bumps. They tell me that even on fair days the newcomer from the west needs a few hours to assure himself that Wellington is not rolling and lurching beneath his feet.

When the lurching subsided, I became aware of three very forceful characters in the city: Peter Fraser, the Prime Minister; Brigadier General Patrick J. Hurley, America's diplomatic representative there; and Little Al, a stoat or ferret. They dominated our visit.

I mean no disrespect to the statesmen, Fraser and Hurley, in bracketing them with Al, the carnivore. It was our own fault that the stoat came into our lives to begin with, and once this force for evil was unleashed, there was no way of recalling it. Also, there was no way of ignoring it. You cannot introduce a killer into a small, select community of travelers and expect things to be the same as they were before. It was a sad day we called on Mr. Whiteacre, senior partner of Whiteacre, Dentice and Company, Limited, land agents, of Wellington, and acquired Little Al for one pound cash.

The error arose out of seagoing tradition and rank sentimentality. When I sailed to Australia from America in convoy, the troops brought the dog Dopey aboard to serve as mascot and bear them company. They figured they would need a four-footed friend at sea. Most sailors feel the same way, and our voyage aboard the *Floating Firecracker* was happier for the presence of the chow dog, Ching, and one rabbit and two monkeys. When we touched at New Zealand, we were bound on a homeward journey that promised to be much lonelier than the other two. Big ships leave America full, but go home fairly empty.

I don't know if you have ever read *The Wind in the Willows,* by Kenneth Grahame. It is a fine book for man or child. In the course of its story the home of Toad (of Toad Hall) is invaded by stoats, ferrets, and weasels, who set themselves up in style and eat the owner's victuals and drink his wines. They are painted as an undesirable element in the community, true, but there is something rakish about their revels and toasts and songs that appeals to the reader. I had been stoat-conscious ever since I read the book. They sounded like good company.

There is another story, *Sredni Vashtar,* by Saki, in which a stoat or ferret is by way of being the hero. He is bloodthirsty, sure enough, but he serves as the friend and ally of a mistreated young boy.

I never realized, when the stoat or ferret went for the jugular vein of the wicked aunt in that tale, that this was the universal policy of stoats or ferrets, and that they never pause to distinguish between good men and evil before leaping. When we added Little Al to the party—he was named for Raymond, to whom he bore a slight resemblance—I thought he would relieve the monotony of shipboard life on the wide Pacific and become attached to us, once he understood that we were neither churchbox-robbers nor child-beaters.

He did become attached to several of us, crew members as well as correspondents, and we still bear the scars. Everything indicated by Grahame and Saki about the anti-social tendencies of the stoat is true. But you have to live through it to find out. I doubt if Saki or Grahame ever shared a small cabin with a stoat for ten days at sea. They would write a little less whimsically if they had.

The way to set about finding a stoat in Wellington, New Zealand, is to inquire at a pet shop, where you will be directed to the office of Mr. Whiteacre, a respectable real estate man who raises stoats and ferrets as a hobby. You will get nowhere, to be sure, unless you scrap your pride and say "weasel" instead of stoat. Then people know what you are talking about. It was a source of much irritation to Little Al's keepers, on board ship, to hear him called a weasel. I didn't have much use for him as a character after a while, God knows, but I did not like to see him cheated of his stoathood.

Mr. Whiteacre brought a stoat into town on one day's notice. Knickerbocker and I called for him. There was a woman client in the office who crooned with rapture over Al's rich brown fur and soft tan belly and general cuteness. She overlooked his red eyes. Then, when Coach Whiteacre turned him loose on the floor and handled him skillfully with a deft lunge of the hand just behind the stoat's shoulders, we thought things promised pretty well. That lunge with the hand looked easy.

"Feed him bread soaked in water, with the water squeezed out, once a day," said his sponsor. "Once a week, give him a piece of raw meat or liver about the size of your thumb. He may soon become a real pet. Or he may not," said Mr. Whiteacre, pocketing the pound note, "depending on your skill with animals."

Pretty confident of our skill with animals, we thanked the coach and set out to do some shopping, carrying Little Al along in a box. We got him a leather harness, inscribed "Allen," and a long leather leash. We got him a leather traveling bag, square and silk-lined, with holes punched in the top for ventilation, and transferred Al to the bag from his box. Later, remembering the ease with which this maneuver was carried out, I realized Al must have been stupefied by the rapid changes in his life. It never worked again, without danger to human life.

With the stoat in his case, we stopped at the bar of the Hotel Wellington to review the situation. I called Coach Whiteacre on the telephone to ask him if the stoat would need a mate on the voyage; this being one of the afterthoughts that occurred to us in the bar. The expert said no.

"He will need nothing," said Whiteacre patiently, "but loving care, bread and water carefully squeezed, and once a week a piece of raw meat or liver about the size of your..."

"Fine," I said, and went back to reassure Knickerbocker. We had an appointment with Mr. Fraser, the Prime Minister, at the same hotel that afternoon, so we checked Al in his case with the girl at the desk in the lobby.

"What is in there?" asked the young lady amiably.

"A pussycat," said Ralph Jordan, who had joined us by now and was too embarrassed to reveal the truth. "Please do not open the case, miss. The little cat is very sensitive."

We redeemed Al a couple of hours later—and it was plain that a change had come over the house's attitude. The girl pointed silently at the traveling case when we asked for it. We had almost reached the door before she called after us, with a peculiar, almost hysterical, break in her voice.

"I don't know what you have in there," she said shrilly, "but that's no pussycat!"

I believe Little Al's red eyes gave off a glow through the holes. At any rate, I know they glowed night after night on shipboard, through the slats in the big new home we ordered for him. Jordan shared a stateroom with the stoat and me. He moved to a room on another deck when we were three nights out. The man was in a cold panic, and admitted it frankly. Little Al moved out a week later. Rather than face the humiliation of being dispossessed by a stoat. I got his cage moved to the boat deck. Only then did the nights become sweet and free of nightmare for those of us who slept below.

Meanwhile, though, we had tried to cultivate our mascot, and one by one he smashed our pink illusions.

The first night out, dumping Al from his case into an empty bathtub before the eyes of a crowded house, I attempted to "handle" him with the subtle lunge I had seen Mr. Whiteacre make. I had on thick gloves, but his teeth went through them and into my thumb, which, come to think of it, was the size of a small piece of raw liver.

When his next move almost carried him over the

edge of the bathtub, the room became empty in five seconds.

The way I got Al back into captivity, then and then-after, was to put his meals inside the cage. He would generally go in after them, following a survey of the outside world.

The second night out he chewed my ankle, the nearest vulnerable spot to hand, and chased Jordan up on a chair. Knickerbocker sneered at what he called our poltroonery and mishandling of a delicate animal, so the following evening Al stalked Knickerbocker and bit him firmly in the rear of the right thigh. The noted authority on animals sailed into his room on the fly, through the connecting bathroom, tore off his pants, and screamed for anti-tetanus treatment.

On the fourth night the stoat caught the fancy of the second steward, who sat in our cabin feeling mellow and watching Al graze on liver.

"Nice kitty," said the steward tenderly, reaching out to pet the red-eyed murderer.

It took us almost a minute to dig Al out of the steward's wrist.

A few days later two confident young blades came into the room with the huge stoat stable they had built to order: John, the ship's joiner, and Howdy Howe, the bellhop, a fugitive from a vaudeville act in Australia. I carefully transferred Al to his new quarters, and we stood back to view the effect, while the stoat nosed along the slats in front of his cage, testing.

"These fellas are easy to handle if you know something about 'em," said Howdy Howe expansively. "I learned about weasels from. . . ."

Little Al's muzzle suddenly passed between two slats, followed by his red eyes and his sinuous neck. Howe stopped short.

"Do you suppose he can get out through there?" asked the retired acrobat, in a strange, choking voice.

I took another look, nodded slowly, and stepped backward. John the joiner simply drew himself up in a corner of the cabin and stood very still. Howdy Howe sprang from the floor to the topmost bunk in a tier of three in a single leap. Little Al came sifting through the bars, and stood in the middle of the room, his ruby eyes moving quickly from left to right.

This was his last public stand. The spell of terror he cast over crew and passenger was now complete. That night, in spite of the fact that I lured the stoat back into his cage with bread and had the slats narrowed, a group of vigilantes met on the deck above, headed by Jordan, and laid their plans. I believe their program was to throw Little Al overboard at night.

If the lynching never materialized, it was because the posse was too timid to close in. Working on this fear, I obtained a compromise—not from love of Herman the Vermin Ermine, as the crew called Little Al, but just for auld lang syne and from a sort of guilt I felt at taking the killer so many thousands of miles from the rabbit holes of his old home near Wellington, New Zealand. His cage was shifted to the top deck, and there he passed the rest of the voyage beneath the sun and the stars. Jangled nerves began to settle, down on *C* deck. Once more songs were heard along the corridor of an evening, and the room stewards moved about with lighter steps, whistling at their work. A sailor took charge of Little Al when we reached port. His plan was to sell him, and if he did so, he made a smart profit—since he got Al for nothing, without strings.

Though the stoat was acquired with the best and most honest of sentimental motives. I will always regret the time and attention he demanded in Wellington, because it gave me less chance to watch the high-spirited performance of General Hurley, the belle of the city.

The general looked good, with his high shock of white hair, his brilliant uniform, and his eyeglasses complete with black ribbon. He appeared to be having a fine time as U. S. Minister to New Zealand, promising help to the natives.

"They loved me, I believe, in my first speeches, of which there was a considerable number," said the general placidly. "My pledges in behalf of tne United States were boundless. While the echoes of a ringing ovation still ricocheted from the walls one evening, I turned to one of the boys and said: 'I seem to have gone over pretty well.'

" 'Why not?' he said. 'You promised them everything but your stock in Richfield Oil.'

"And I had," said the general, beaming. "I had. They struck me as fine people, deserving of the best there was."

It came home to Hurley reasonably soon, however, that the New Zealanders had no more disposition to be "saved" than the Australians. Furthermore, they were much less concerned than Australia about the prospects of being invaded. Those prospects were considered good, at first, by Australians and Americans. New Zealand commanded the Pacific supply route.

"If they don't go for us," I heard an Australian cabinet minister say in March, "they will most likely go for New Zealand."

This thought did not disturb New Zealanders at all, and when General Hurley perceived this, he began to feel somewhat confined. It narrowed the scope of his eloquence. It chafed him. When I saw him in Wellington, he was commencing to mutter, with dignified ardor, about his craving for action.

"I must lead troops into battle again," said Hoover's

symmetrical war secretary, pacing the floor. "That is the need I feel."

If the general also felt the need of a straight man to balance this role, he found him in Mr. Heenan, head of the government's information service. Mr. Heenan supplemented each of the general's outbursts, when they reached a pause indicating a paragraph, with a few grave remarks about Hurley's value to New Zealand, the importance of his job there, and the admiration the people and the government felt for him. The general would then shoot Mr. Heenan a gracious smile of acknowledgment.

"You see how I am torn," he said, continuing to pace the carpet.

There was not much real doubt, though, that the call of action pulled the general more strongly. Before he was sent to New Zealand, he had done a good job—considering Japan's jealous alertness and the strength of her blockade—of running supplies to Bataan and Corregidor from Australia. He had even run himself through the blockade a couple of times, and out again. He was in Darwin the day of the first great bombing of February 19, and the fact that he picked up a scalp wound from shrapnel did not dampen his warlike spirit in the least.

The general, then, was restless in New Zealand as

well as highly scenic. Once he detected the self-reliance
of New Zealand's people, and their perfect willingness
to take care of themselves, there was nothing to hold
a Hurley in Wellington; and, sure enough, a few weeks
after our visit, he was out of there, hitching a ride with
Prime Minister Fraser when the latter paid a quick
call on the United States.

"At heart," said the general, by way of explaining
his debouchement, "I am the fighter type—a pirate."

The solid courage and matter-of-factness which Hurley found in New Zealand—which cramped his style to
some extent—was represented pretty well by Fraser
himself. The Prime Minister was a big, frosty-powed,
quiet Scotsman, up from the mines. His diplomatic
manner was suave enough, but there was ruggedness
behind it, and a sharp quality, too, which leaped into
view one day at a meeting he had with some American
reporters.

We were sitting over tea, scones, and sandwiches,
the trimmings without which no burgess of that stoutly
Anglican country can confer and feel completely
dressed. One correspondent, stationed in Wellington,
had a complaint to make—about censorship, naturally.
Why didn't New Zealand censors cooperate with the
American censor under Vice-Admiral Robert Ghormley?

"They do," said Fraser, lifting his teacup.

"Not properly. It causes a lot of dissatisfaction. Of course, if you want to risk that. . . ."

"Well?" said Fraser, his chin coming forward.

"Well," floundered the reporter, "I mean, if you didn't have American help, you know. . . ."

"We would struggle along without it," said Fraser dryly.

He then explained what he did hope and expect from America—"and the people too, I'm sure I speak for them all." It was a slightly different pattern of thought from the ones we had encountered. It meshed cleanly, as things turned out, with the purpose of Ghormley and the American troops who had just followed him to New Zealand. These troops were Marines, and the next we heard of them, they were on the beaches of the Solomon Islands.

I think there is no doubt that the blurred line dividing the command of General MacArthur from that of Ghormley, under Admiral Nimitz at Pearl Harbor, led to confusion in the Southwest Pacific. It may have marred the efficiency of some of the Allied operations. Certainly there were conflicting opinions here and there as to which Japanese-held objective to strike first.

Fraser, at the time, was not concerned with any such

subdivisions of the general purpose. He merely described that purpose, as he and New Zealand saw it—to strike, not defend.

"New Zealand has never asked to be defended," said the Scotsman soberly. "We don't understand the war that way. If we were attacked, we would defend ourselves to the death. But that's not the first idea. The first idea is that this country should be—we want it to be—a base for attack on the enemy. We won't win unless we attack him."

New Zealand's own soldiery was still concentrated in the Middle East, where it had been sent before the Japanese began the Pacific war. The African record of the New Zealanders, including the native Maori troops, has been brilliant all the way, and the people at home can cite every line of it.

There was no evidence, however, that they had any more notion than Peter Fraser of recalling the troops for their own defense. Travelers say, and the New Zealanders do not deny, that the country is closer to England in thought and custom than Australia is, more consciously a part of the Empire. I can't draw any such spacious conclusion as that, on the strength of a three-day visit, without fracturing the bylaws of the Deep Thinkers lodge. But the people of New Zealand are sturdy and friendly and apparently fearless for their own safety, and if they can dispense with the protection and succor of General Pat Hurley, as seems to be the case, they are obviously capable of standing alone.

That appeared to be the conclusion the general came to, and he acted upon it without delay.

XXIII

Homeward: the Odd Page

OUTWARD bound, to Britain, Africa, Asia, Australia, and the islands of the South Pacific, our troopships go laden with men under arms, and one floating city is much like another. There are the same bunks in triple tiers, the same long shuffling processions to mess, the same drills, the same blacked-out decks by night, the same ceremonies and services, the same card games and forums, the same alarms and rumors and signs of submarines, the same orders and speeches by commanding officers that roll metallically down the deckway from the loudspeaker; always, I guess, there is the same feeling of adventure and nervous excitement and groping anticipation.

I read a newspaper story in the autumn of 1942 that told about the first large troop convoy to reach New Zealand. It was our Australian convoy of the previous winter all over again, with the slightest of variations. There was even a "first man off"—a luckier soldier than our Sergeant B., to be sure, since he did manage to get off first, with the right stage effects.

When those same ships roll home again, to pick up fresh loads, the voyage is something else entirely. No two homebound cargoes are alike. The wartime life of every transport ship is a page with two sides, and the odd side tells strange stories, bright or grimy, romantic or medium dull, but never the same.

The big ship that took us to Australia had just steamed home from Samoa with the first roundup of war waifs and refugees from the south seas—a thousand of them, all women and children, with the round sum of eighty prostitutes included in the company. The even page of the log took her south again with several thousand troops bound for war, and I know she was expecting to carry back the first wounded, men and women alike, of the Java and Philippine campaigns.

"That's what we expect," said Captain Spencer, the transport surgeon, "but God knows what we'll get: maybe Hirohito and the Jap general staff. We'll have the sulfa ready, and the irons too."

Now, on the vessel that took us northeast from Australia and New Zealand and the Tasman Sea, we had a mixed bag. It was a ship re-patterned for soldiers, with three, six, and nine beds to a room, but the only sizable consignment of troops we carried in this direction were blue-clad flying cadets from the Anzac countries, bound for training in America. They were eager, cheerful youngsters. They could sing, and almost always did. One of them played the harmonica like a virtuoso. As soon as this became known, my mouth-organ was transferred by stealth from me to him, and spirits rose, I heard it said, all over the ship.

For the rest, we had the wife of a Dutch admiral and her son and daughter; two Dutch officers and their families; an American naval ensign from the submarine service, headed home on leave, and another from the PT boats of the Philippines, on the same errand; the New Zealand delegate of General Motors, willing to argue far into the night that production would win the war; and eight army nurses who escaped from Corregidor by plane just a week before the Philippine fortress fell.

We had sailed with them a day or two before we realized that more than half of these eight girls were still suffering from the last effects of shock: true deadening shock that left them apathetic and vague-eyed, with intervals of sudden painful reaction when some finger of chance touched an unhealed nerve.

A plane was sighted our second day out. It was a friendly plane, as most of the crew and passengers, matter-of-fact and healthy, guessed from the start. It produced a convulsive recoil, a jittery fright, among the nurses—four of whom had taken the full impact of the bloody Bataan campaign, had worked under bombing for fifteen weeks, had never been out of sight or sound of enemy aircraft from Christmas Day till the final bombardment of the rocky fort in Manila Bay.

Their hard-bought shell of resistance melted away during two months of peace and safety and convalescence in Australia, and the unexpected sight of one plane caught them offguard, with the old wounds exposed. It needed something like the little isolated hysteria of these women to tell us what the last days of Bataan were like. Words, such as Americans read in their newspapers in April and May of 1942, are ineffectual and quickly taken for granted.

Nobody saw the final day on Bataan but the Japanese and the men of our garrison, dead or imprisoned, and a few fugitives who swam or were ferried to Corregidor under three hours of dive-bombing attack, while dynamite sent guns and munitions dumps roaring skyward on the beach behind them.

"I thought it was the end of the world," said Dorothea Daley. Yet Daley, grave, snub-nosed little nurse from Hamilton, Missouri, missed half of what happened in this wild retreat because she fell asleep from exhaustion whenever the fugitive caravan paused for a few minutes in its course.

Daley married a soldier on Bataan. They knew a few days' happiness together at the hospital in the jungle near the little coastal village of Cabcaben, living outdoors, sleeping on blankets on the ground, before her husband returned to the lines, to be captured with the rest of the Army when the Japanese broke through on April 8 and overran the peninsula.

Another nurse, Ressa Jenkins, a dark-skinned girl from the Great Smoky Mountain region of Tennessee, left a sister behind in the Philippines. Only half of the Army's eighty-five nurses escaped, in fact—twenty of them were in a Catalina flying boat that took off from the waters of Manila Bay, near Cavité, just one week before General Jonathan R. Wainwright surrendered Corregidor. Japanese shellfire was kicking chips from the rocks of Corregidor on the night they left, and a Zero plane followed them far out to sea on the last lap of their flight, from Mindanao to Darwin.

As the days passed on our homeward voyage, the nurses slowly recovered their interest in life. They began to talk, haltingly at first, about Bataan, and we saw that there was something more than the memory of bombs and shells in their feeling about it; more, also, than the thought of those who were left behind. They had never understood, and did not yet understand, why no help was sent to the Philippines.

They took Bataan's isolation harder, perhaps, than most of the men who fought there. They were not much concerned with the rest of the world at war. This was the battle into which chance dropped them—

a bitter, bloody, tragic battle, that found them ready to do their work well and bravely but always with confidence, till the last few days, that help would come. It seemed impossible to them that men who suffered as these nurses saw them suffer, in their first taste of war, would not be saved or supported. The hell of Bataan was their only reality for four months; yet they never could bring themselves to believe fully in its implications.

Juanita Redmond read to us from her diary, an entry for January: "Our morale is very high because we hear there is a 200-mile-long convoy coming in. God speed the day."

They clung to such beliefs from start to finish, and their reaction was the more bitter for it. Daley, on April 8, when the nurses were ordered to evacuate their hospital, did not understand what had happened. A doctor told her the lines had broken and that Jap scouts and snipers were already in Cabcaben, two kilometers away. She simply shook her head numbly and climbed aboard the garbage truck that was to take her and a few others to the port of Marivales. Not even the sight of patients and doctors clustering around the nurses, with messages for their families at home, made the scene real to her.

Earlier in the campaign these women sang songs they wrote to fit the occasion. The fighting was still well to the north of them, and there was a rueful but humorous zest in their singing:

>"Dig those foxholes deeper, Doug,
>Dig down, dig down,
>Dig those foxholes deeper, Doug,
>Dig 'em all the way.
>Bombs gonna fall all night,
>Bombs gonna fall all day,
>So dig those foxholes deeper, Doug,
>The Nips are on their way.
>
>When's that convoy coming in,
>Franklin, Franklin?
>When's that convoy coming in,
>Franklin D., old man?
>Gonna sweat all night,
>Gonna sweat all day,
>We'll sweat that convoy coming in
>Till she hits the bay."

Another, written to the tune of *Missouri Waltz* by the same girl, Helen Summers, of Boston, told of the jungle life they led:

>"Way out in Bataan, when we were in the A.N.C.,
>Ate two meals per day and drank diluted ginger tea,
>We stood in the chow line,

After the day's grind,
And caribao stew
Was our daily menu.
Sitting on a rock and bathing in a mountain stream,
Wish we could awake and find it only just a dream,
But for the duration,
We'll pretend it's a vacation,
And see it through."

These nurses enlisted in peacetime in the *A.N.C.*, the Army Nurse Corps. For some of them it was romance and escape of a sort. They had a gay time in prewar Manila, with normal hours of duty and dancing and dates in the evening. Bataan and bombs were not on the program. The rancid little Bataan River was beyond the power of their imaginations even on the day when the Japanese wiped out the American air force within a few hours of Pearl Harbor and the nurses found themselves tending men wounded in battle for the first time.

Things moved so fast after that that they never quite caught up. Four months to the day after the blasting of Clark Field, they were rattling in trucks and wagons by night down a rutted road toward the last refuge of Corregidor, while snipers' bullets whistled around them, and the earth shook with the sacrifice of our dynamited munitions, and children were run down by the wheels of the fugitive traffic that clogged the narrow way through the jungle.

While Bataan held, the nurses from Manila worked in two outdoor hospitals at the foot of the peninsula. Shielded by burlap hangings, they bathed in the chlorinated river water. They ate rice and the meat of the caribao, the Philippine water buffalo, till the caribao ran out. Then they ate horse and rice or mule and rice. Mule made the best eating of the three.

Daley and Eunice Hatchett, from Texas, worked at Hospital No. 2, near Cabcaben. They had thirty-six hundred beds and, at the finish, seven thousand patients, military and civilian. Miss Hatchett—Hatch— tended two hundred and sixty patients at once. This hospital was not hit by the Japanese planes. The other hospital, No. 1, at Little Baguio, was struck twice —the second time deliberately, according to Miss Redmond, who worked there.

Little Baguio was where the wounded were sent first. It was there the surgeons discovered a new treatment for gangrene, when their supply of sulfa medicines was exhausted. Wounds were opened, cleaned, incised, and exposed to the sun, without dressing. This produced better results, we heard, than sulfa.

The Japanese bombed the hospital late in March. They apologized for this raid by radio, from Manila, calling it a mistake. However, their planes returned at

9:15 in the morning of April 3 and smashed the place to bits. Patients were blown into trees. Arms and legs hung from branches. Beds, sheets, and mattresses were scattered all over the jungle. In the orthopedic section, where men with broken limbs were tied up in plaster casts, an attendant ran along cutting the ropes so the patients could roll off the beds and take shelter beneath them.

The last American lines on Bataan broke on April 8. All eighty-five nurses on the mainland were evacuated by order, and reached the little port of Marivales, opposite Corregidor, just twenty-five minutes after the formal surrender of Bataan on the morning of April 9. The harbor steamer *Mitchel* took them to the island fort, under dive-bombing all the way, and there Daley remembered how the nurses, with no clothes but those they wore, were issued men's underwear from the army stores—the shorts ranging in color from pink to purple.

"I was lucky, I got white ones," she said.

They also were issued the first real cigarettes they had seen in weeks. The "Bataan cigarette" was made of bamboo leaves wrapped in toilet paper.

The nurses lived in the tunnels of Corregidor for three weeks, while the Japs bombarded Wainwright's last position. They ate well and regularly now. Daley gained back half of the thirty pounds she had lost on Bataan. At 6 P.M., April 29, twenty nurses were called to a meeting by the chief nurse, Captain Davis, who told them they were leaving for Australia that night. Another group of twenty escaped later in the week, making the total not quite half of the nurses on Corregidor. There were only two Catalinas available for each flight. The women who went were selected, not by lot, but in consideration of age, dependents, and other special circumstances. One of them, wife of an officer, was pregnant.

A special priority list was drawn up in case either of the planes failed to get off.

The nurses were told to say nothing to anyone on the island; to dispense with good-bys. But everyone knew. Once more they were surrounded by people giving them messages for families at home. General Wainwright came to the docks to see them off. They were carried by PT boats to a point about two hundred yards off the Cavité shore—and there, in the darkness, they rendezvoused with the Catalinas that flew them to Mindanao and finally to Darwin. Hatch remembered best the long, dragging takeoff from Mindanao, and the reason for it. The plane rode the water for three miles before it rose. The reason was a stowaway, hidden in the toilet astern.

"He was a little, pimply-faced soldier in the air corps," said Hatch. "He was so happy to be out of the Islands. He said he wouldn't get more than a year from the court martial, and then he'd be free to nght the Japs again. I couldn't help sympathizing with him."

The stowaway was arrested in Australia. Hatch never did hear how he made out with the court martial.

The women had a final fright before they reached their goal. The plane's pilot rode into the dawn to find himself over the Japanese base of Koepang, in Timor. He executed a rapid left turn. A few hours later he came down in Darwin, and that night the nurses saw movies outdoors and were serenaded by the South Dakota band.

It was in Darwin that Miss Redmond's fiancé, an air force pilot, had been killed in an accidental crash.

Summer days are long and quiet on the Pacific. Sometimes we read. Sometimes we slept. Sometimes we walked the boat deck, and passed the time of day with Little Al, the stoat, who was now hating people's guts in the open air instead of in a cabin below.

Sometimes we listened to another side of the story of Bataan. Colonel George S. Clark was the last combat officer to leave Corregidor before its fall, carrying dispatches from General Wainwright. He was also in command of the Fifty-Seventh Philippine Scouts, who held our right flank in the first important Japanese land attack of the Bataan campaign—the attack on the Abucay line, on the night of January 4.

This assault gave American troops their first taste of Japanese fighting. It showed them that the enemy had thrown the book of rules away. It was a hodge-podge of noise, mass suicide, mass charges, subtle infiltration, and fear psychology. It hurled its chief strength against Clark's position on the right, along the eastern shore of Bataan. Colonel John M. Doyle's Forty-fifth Scouts held the left, on the other side of the peninsula. These two regiments were the only regular Army units on the line. The center was held by the Philippine Army.

The Japs began by raising a hullabaloo with drums, firecrackers, and tiny mortars which did no damage but set up a gruesome racket—which was the whole purpose of the opening maneuver. Their next move was to send a wave of a thousand men into the open between the lines, shooting as they came, to draw the fire of the Americans and reveal our positions. Other waves of men followed the first. Two or three hundred Japs fell dead out of each thousand so delegated.

Clark had studded his outer line with land mines. Here the Japanese gave their second demonstration of suicide strategy. Instead of exploding the mines by artillery fire, they sent out new lines of men, a flesh-and-blood sacrifice, to do the job. Each man, as he found a mine, shouted *"Banzai!"* and leaped full upon it. When all the mines were exploded, Jap troops surged forward over the bodies of their own dead. They repeated the formula when they came to our barbed wire. The next suicide detail threw itself upon the wire with the same shrill yells of *"Banzai!"*, and formed another bridge of dead.

Our artillery mowed them down in clusters that night. The Japs fell back at last; far back, as was their custom, leaving vast stretches of no man's land where the Philippine farmers resumed the tilling of the ground by day. Clark, surveying the field on the morning of January 5, estimated Japanese losses in dead and abandoned at fifty to one of his own.

"And that's conservative," he said. "Some of my officers called it two or three hundred to one."

Yet the attack had achieved its first purpose: of filtering scores of snipers through our lines. These men were far more magnificently equipped than the average Jap soldier—fine clothing, plenty of food, flawless camouflage, and a thousand rounds of ammunition for each .27 caliber rifle. Sometimes as many as eight of them manned one tree. They never risked notice by swinging a gun barrel to get a new bead. If you crossed a sniper's line of fire, his gun spoke—walking between the set lines of fire, you might go right up the tree itself.

By night, the snipers doubled in psychology. The natives of Luzon defer to a special corps of spirits, against whom they barricade their doors at night. The Jap sniper in his tree behind the American lines could impersonate these spirits with skill, playing upon the nerves and superstitions of the natives with a high, wailing cry that rose and fell in the night. Clark, a veteran of the Philippines, identified the words of the cry: *"Patay na ikaw!"*, the gist of them being "Now you are going to die!"

For Clark, the campaign reached a serio-comic climax some weeks later, far down the peninsula on our last defense line, when the nightly ration of horse and rice was doled out. Clark was halfway through his meal when a quartermaster officer said:

"We're eating Dollar tonight, colonel."

Dollar was Clark's horse. The colonel put down his knife and ate no more.

We sighted land in the morning. By noon we stood off port, looking at America, a dark bulk dappled with sunshine. The cadets from Australia and New Zealand were easy marks under this new excitement, sitting targets for any American passenger who wanted to tell them about Texas or California or Philadelphia or La-grange, Indiana. And every American passenger did. The sight of home after a long voyage unfailingly acts upon the ocean pilgrim as a bottle of wine upon a man with an empty stomach.

The nurses from Bataan planned a shopping tour. Most of them still had no clothes but their khaki coveralls, the ones they wore in the jungle, and a single blue Australian uniform apiece.

Pretty soon we were in the town, and then we discovered what will be the first two impulses of every Yank who comes home from the Pacific when the war is over. He will want to buy up all the cigarettes in sight, and he will want to seize a telephone and call long distance. The tobacco dealers had better be ready. So had Central.

Notes

NOTE 1 (chapter 1, page 12): If I were haled into court, perish the thought, on charges of plagiarism in the third to fifth degrees, inclusive, and literary peculation in fee simple, with overtones of lèse-majesté, in connection with the use of the phrase "typewriter strategist"—well, I would confound counsel for the plaintiff with six bales of affidavits and eleven or twelve witnesses of mixed denominations, all testifying that I put those words on paper on July 23, 1942, along about milking time.

The President of the United States gave the phrase wide currency by employing it in a speech in October of the same year. There is no more gifted wordsmith and phrasewright in action than the President. He is welcome to "typewriter strategist," if he needs it, which I doubt. I stand by with my affidavits and my witnesses (who are costing me $9 a day in rye alone) just in case some outsider, some officious bounder pretending to uphold the public weal, charges me with embezzlement from Mr. Roosevelt and his staff of literary spooks.

I hope I don't have to go to court, though. If the case attracted attention, seven men and women would straightway step forward and start pelting me with their own affidavits, proving that they thought of "typewriter strategist" in 1894. I would then have to get my witnesses to reverse themselves and swear I was in Bermuda, shooting Kelly pool, at the time of the crime.

NOTE 2 (chapter 5, page 60): The author speaks glibly of platypuses, but the fact is he did not see any. Nor, though he spent some time on Cape York and the Darwin peninsula and the waters thereabout, did he see any of the following zoological marvels, said to infest the region: the dingo, the flying fox, or fruit bat; the mud skipper, or tree-climbing fish; the dugong, or sea-cow, thought to have suggested the mermaid to early navigators; the quarter-ton clam; the erne; and the erne's prey, the venomous sea snake.

I did see koala bears, wallabies, and carpet snakes. The most memorable animal I beheld in the Southwest Pacific was a rat crossing a road in New Guinea, a rat the size of a small pony. If you put a saddle on this specimen, and paid the entry fee, you could run him in the Kentucky Derby.

NOTE 3 (end of chapter 11): There is much I've left unsaid about the merits of certain American war planes that were active in the Pacific at the start of the fighting there. This is not from lack of evidence; nearly every pilot I saw had something to say about our pursuit planes powered by the Allison motor, the first P-40's and P-39's, and very little of what they said, comparing these ships to the Japanese Zero for the purposes in hand, was favorable.

However, I see no point in belaboring the subject in this book. I could speak only as a general reporter, not as a technician or qualified authority. Besides, I think the debates of the last year, although ill-tempered and cross-purposed in the main, have already served the most useful possible end: that of circulating all available information and setting us on the right track.

It's enough to say here that what I saw, heard, and inferred about our war planes in the Pacific coincides almost exactly with what America's Office of War Information (insofar as it covered the same ground) reported in October, 1942—briefly, that our early fighter planes did not perform as well as the Japanese ships at high altitudes, and that three of our bomber planes (the B-25 and B-26, mediums, and the B-17 or Flying Fortress, heavy) were by far the best of their kinds in that area at that time.

NOTE 4 (end of chapter 15): This is the postscript to the post-log of the *Floating Firecracker:* she was torpedoed and sunk in the Pacific a few weeks after our voyage to New Guinea. I learned this after returning home. No lives were lost, all hands being rescued by units of the Royal Australian Air Force soon after the sinking; which is a pretty sure indication that she carried no drums of high octane gasoline and no bombs, restless or otherwise, on her last journey.

NOTE 5 (chapter 16, page 187): The details of battles like Milne Bay, when they begin to sift through the censor's fences, make a special and warmly interesting sort of reading for any soldier or reporter who has traveled widely over a given battle area—alumni bulletin stuff, telling him about the doings of his old acquaintances in the great world.

There were American units at Milne Bay, as well as Australians, and the Yanks did some of the best fighting that was done there in the rout of the Japanese. There was an anti-aircraft outfit with which I sailed to Australia in convoy, at a time when the troops were green and untried, fresh from schools and farms and office jobs at home, wondering to themselves what they would do under fire. In the test, they worked with murderously good effect. So did another outfit, whose trail I crossed months before in the lonely wilderness of Darwin—the XX Engineers, the admiration of every Yank and Digger in the Darwin neighborhood for the skill and speed with which they carved airfields out of the jungle. They were outstanding heroes at Milne Bay when the moment came to drop their tools and shoot.

NOTE 6 (chapter 17, page 200): I doubt if any place in the world at war can equal Australia for resistance to the encroachments of the Military. For instance, the Military considered Bluey Truscott a flight lieutenant (leftenant) when he returned to England to serve with the Royal Australian Air Force, and the People, composed very largely of football fans, considered him a Squadron Leader who was being short-changed by the Military.

The People's choices in Parliament argued this case for two weeks. Bluey became a Squadron Leader. It is enough to make the squire of Berchtesgaden spin like a pinwheel with disgust and confusion.

NOTE 7 (end of chapter 18): The seven deadly young men deserve a footnote, if only to show what is required of flyers in the Pacific. They must be combinations of Eddie Rickenbacker and the Admirable Crichton, with the best features of Daniel Boone thrown in. And most of them are. Raised in a land of de luxe sedans and central heating, in the flower of the Electric Icebox Era, it is startling to see how deftly and ruggedly American airmen defeat the trackless jungle, when they fall in its lap from the sky, and subdue the hazards of starvation, fever, heat, and wilderness.

Sometimes they are shot down. Sometimes weather, or the unpredictable delays of a bombing mission or air fight, will leave them far from home with their fuel tanks empty. If they reach the ground or sea alive, they square off against nature's wildest handiwork with nothing more than a frail life raft, a pocketful of concentrated rations, a revolver, a small compass, and a knife. It's different, I heard one pilot say with powerful restraint, from White Plains, N. Y. It took the man from White Plains and his crew a full day to cut one mile of path through tropic undergrowth with their knives.

Yet they turn up. Hatch and Seffern turned up. Bearded, tattered, and thin, they walked into Port Moresby from opposite directions on a late summer day many weeks after our flight over Lae. This time the luck of the skies had deserted them. On another flight in the New Guinea region, both their ships—Seffern had his own plane by now—were knocked out by storm and shortage of fuel. Hatch and his crew came down off the coast, made land, and plowed a hundred and fifty miles to the safety of Moresby, through country controlled and in some parts occupied by Japs.

I'd written a letter to Hatch's mother, when he was first reported missing, full of the usual vague comforts and obscure reassurances. If I didn't feel sure of the truth of what I said, I underestimated Hatch. He came in, and brought his men with him.

As for Seffern, the lean, lounging wisecracking youth from Wisconsin, he tramped through the jungle for twenty days—and walked in gaunt but grinning. Seffern and his crew had bailed out from 13,000 feet, which made me think uneasily back to my own ride without a parachute. Hatch, a nonchalant fellow, had not mentioned all the possibilities.

One of the men who jumped from Seffern's plane, two and a half miles above the earth—and I cite him to show that even a war correspondent can be tough—was Vern Haugland, of the Associated Press, a tall, thin, retiring young man with a shy smile. I heard people say he looked like a school teacher. He certainly didn't look rugged. Yet Haugland endured the wilderness for nearly fifty days, alone much of the time and with his slim body racked by fever.

NOTE 8 (chapter 20, page 227): If you don't think a matter of low doorknobs can start a brawl among restless soldiers, consider the case—it came about in October, 1942—of the Australian private who was killed in a fight that started over the way American soldiers wear their neckties. A Yank was reprimanded by M.P.'s in a public park in Australia, for not tucking his tie in at the shirt. When the M.P.'s moved on, two Diggers began to kid the Yank about etiquette. Diggers are rough kidders. Two more Americans joined the first, and one of the Australians was stabbed to death and another wounded in the shambles that followed.

Glossary

This lexicon, a superficial one, is designed simply to give an idea of the range and flavor of the slang the Australians use, more especially the Australian soldiers. Considering that the population of the entire country is about the same as New York City's, Australians are probably the busiest and most vigorous slangsters in the English-speaking world.

Youth may account for this. Australia is a younger country than the United States. The United States, in turn, is far younger than England, and your reading will tell you—or your ears, if they have the chance—that American slang is far lustier and more abundant than the pinched, settled slang of the British Isles.

Some of the words and phrases in this list derive from the old rhyming slang I spoke of in Chapter 20, and are so identified by the letters (r.s.). Another glossary of Australian slang, slightly different in content from this one and a very good one, appears in the Pocket Guide to Australia printed for American soldiers and sailors by the War and Navy Departments.

One more point: there are words here which are heard,

which even originated elsewhere, in England or America, for instance. I use them only when they are standard in Australia and New Zealand and firmly identified with the common speech of those countries.

Crackers......crazy, screwy, nuts.

Bonzer......fine, great, exceptionally good.

Dinkum......real, authentic. The "dinkum oil" is the straight goods.

Beaut......good, swell.

Crook......bad, lousy. "My head feels crook to-day."

Cow......heel, bum, no-good.

Wowser......stuffed shirt, bluenose.

Cobber......pal, chum.

Bastard......fine guy, good egg.

Nark......rat, squealer.

Yank, Fitzroy Yank......dude. "Yank," of course, is also applied to all Americans, northern and southern.

Collins Street Squatter......Melbourn localism for street loafer, drug store cowboy.

Skite......boast, brag.

Graft......work hard.

Ta......thanks.

'Bye-o......good-by.

Ta-ta......good-by.

Sarvo......this afternoon.

Dirty Gertie—three-thirty (r.s.).

Sheila......girl, babe, *Sninny* has the same meaning.

Trouble (and strife)......wife (r.s.)

Cheese (and kisses)......also means wife, or Mrs. A more affectionate term, used in the earlier stages of marriage (r.s.).

Smooge......pet, neck, pitch woo.

Pot and pan......old man, man of the house (r.s.).

Abo......aboriginal native of Australia.

Lubra, Mary, gin......aboriginal woman.

Plates of meat......feet (r.s.).

Lump of lead......head (r.s.).

Fiddle (and flute)......suit (r.s.).

Sky (rocket)......pocket (r.s.).

Tucker......food.

Pudding......dessert.

Billy......tin can for boiling tea.

Jimmy Skinner......dinner (r.s.).

Duke (of York)......hand. This universal slang word also originated in rhyming slang, since "Duke of York" once meant "fork."

Milk bar......soda fountain.

Rubadub, or rubadedub......pub, saloon (r.s.).

Shout......treat, as in buying drinks.

Shickered......drunk.

Pig's ear......beer (r.s.).

Plonk......low-grade wine.

Whacks......sharing the cost, Dutch treat.

Shivoo......party.

Beano......de luxe party.

Joes (Joe Blakes)......shakes, blues (r.s.).

In......even number, as in dice.

Out......odd number.

Flick........movie.

Oscar (Ash)......money, cash (r.s.).

Bees (and honey)......money (r.s.).

Quid......pound note.

Copper......penny.

Trey, treybit......threepence.

Zack, saxer......sixpence.

Bob, deener......shilling.

Dollar......five shillings.

Oxford (collar)......dollar (r.s.).

Stager......showoff, grandstand player.

Offsider......counterpart (from Australian football.

Mark......high leap (from Australian football). Mark also means "favorite" in the jargon of the racetrack bookmakers.

Barrack......cheer, applaud, root.

Gee......racehorse.

Moke......horse.

Buckley's Chance......long shot.

Boko......nose.

Bluey......"Red," red-haired man.

John......policeman, cop.

Sister......title of a trained nurse.

Cocky......farmer.

Stockman......rancher.

Muttonjack......sheep-hand.

Bush, outback......the wild country, also "the sticks."

Never Never, bugger-all......the desert.

Joe Anna......piano (r.s.).

God stone the crows......well, well.

CPSIA information can be obtained at www.ICGtesting.com
Printed in the USA
BVOW070802030513

319776BV00002B/2/P